MIRROR

NATASHA SYNESSIOS

KINOfiles Film Companion 6

I.B.Tauris *Publishers*
LONDON • NEW YORK

Published in 2001 by I.B.Tauris & Co Ltd,
6 Salem Road, London W2 4BU
175 Fifth Avenue, New York NY 10010
www.ibtauris.com

In the United States of America and in Canada distributed by
St. Martin's Press, 175 Fifth Avenue, New York NY 10010

ISBN 1 86064 521 6

A full CIP record for this book is available from the British Library
A full CIP record for this book is available from the Library of Congress

Library of Congress catalog card: available

Typeset in Monotype Calisto by Ewan Smith, London
Printed and bound in Great Britain by MPG Books Ltd, Bodmin

Contents

Illustrations

Acknowledgements

I wish to thank Marina Tarkovskaia for her friendship, generosity and trust over the past nine years. I am especially indebted to her for the illustrations in this book. Thanks are also due to: Rima Karpova, who has provided invaluable help and advice during my frequent forays into the Russian archives; Charles de Brantes at the Institut Tarkovski in Paris, for sharing treasures from his archives with me. I am extremely grateful to Julian Graffy for his encouragement and practical help in giving order to a chaotic first draft. Finally I want to thank Richard Taylor and Philippa Brewster; through their support and enthusiasm they have helped to make writing this book a pleasure.

Production Credits

Production company: Mosfilm, Creative Unit 4
Screenplay: Andrei Tarkovsky, Alexander Misharin
Director: Andrei Tarkovsky
Director of photography: Georgi Rerberg
Art direction: Nikolai Dvigubsky
Composer: Eduard Artemiev
Additional music: Johann Sebastian Bach, Giovanni Pergolesi, Henry Purcell
Sound: Semion Litvinov
Producer: E. Vaisberg
Production manager: Iuri Kushnerev
Assistant directors: Larisa Tarkovskaia, V. Kharchenko, Maria Chugunova
Camera operators: A. Nikolaev, I. Shtanko
Editor: Liudmila Feiginova
Lighting: V. Gusev
Sets: A. Merkulov
Special effects: Iuri Potapov
Costumes: Nina Fomina
Make-up: Vera Rudina
USSR release: 7 March 1975
UK release: 17 April 1980
Length: 106 minutes, 11 parts, 2966 metres
Colour and black and white

Cast

Margarita Terekhova	Maria (Masha, Marusia), Alexei's mother and Natalia, Alexei's wife
Maria Tarkovskaia	Alexei's mother as an old woman
Filipp Iankovsky	Alexei, aged five
Ignat Daniltsev	Alexei (Alesha), aged twelve and Ignat, Alexei's son, aged twelve
Oleg Iankovsky	Alexei's father
Nikolai Grinko	Ivan Gavrilovich, Maria's boss at the printing works
Alla Demidova	Elizaveta Pavlovna (Liza), Maria's colleague at the printing works
Iuri Nazarov	military instructor
Anatoli Solonitsyn	a country doctor in first episode
Larisa Tarkovskaia	Nadezhda Petrovna, a rich doctor's wife
Olga Kizilova	girl with red hair
Tamara Ogorodnikova	woman to whom Ignat reads Pushkin letter
Narrator	Innokenti Smoktunovsky

Poems read by the author, Arseni Tarkovsky

Note on Transliteration

Transliteration from the Cyrillic to the Latin alphabet is a perennial problem for writers on Russian subjects. I have opted for a dual system: in the text I have used the Library of Congress system (without diacritics), but I have broken from this system (a) when a Russian name has a clear English version (e.g. Maria instead of Mariia, Alexander instead of Aleksandr); (b) when a Russian name has an accepted English spelling, or when Russian names are of Germanic origin (e.g. Yeltsin instead of Eltsin, Eisenstein instead of Eizenshtein); (c) when a Russian surname ends in -ii or -yi this is replaced by a single -y (e.g. Trotsky instead of Trotskii), and all Christian names end in a single -i. In the scholarly apparatus I have adhered to the Library of Congress system (with diacritics) for the specialist.

This book is dedicated to Alekos Papagos,
for his unfailing love and support

1. Maria Tarkovskaia with her children, Andrei and Marina in Ignatievo, summer 1935. (Photograph: Lev Gornung)

1. Introduction

Mirror occupies a very important place in Andrei Tarkovsky's life and career. It is the fourth of his seven feature films, and it stands at the centre of his cinematic output, separating the three films that preceded it from the three that followed, in more ways than mere numerical calculation. *Mirror* is the culmination and distillation of *Ivan's Childhood* [Ivanovo detstvo, 1962], *Andrei Rublev* [Andrei Rublev, 1966] and *Solaris* [Soliaris, 1972]. It gathers the themes they explored – childhood, war, the artist's responsibility and his struggle, the human being's doubt, guilt and atonement – into one richly textured and resonant universe. It also concludes an aesthetic and emotional cycle of Tarkovsky's artistic expression, and heralds a new direction, one which he pursues in his last three films, *Stalker* [Stalker, 1979], *Nostalgia* [Nostalghia, 1983] and *The Sacrifice* [Offret, 1986]. *Mirror* is, in many ways, Tarkovsky's most unfettered and inspired testimony to the existence of grace and harmony, faith and reconciliation, in a flawed and terrifying world, and a fraught and confused personal life. The three films that followed it, and which represent a trilogy of sorts, sound an increasingly desperate note in this regard. Although they all posit faith, in each successive one that faith becomes more studied, as their protagonists resort to extreme means in order to communicate their vision of a disjointed world – a world which, they believe, can be put right only through self-sacrifice. Nature, the central element of *Mirror*, also goes through a transformation in the last three films. It will never again possess the fecundity and potency it once had. In *Stalker* it is overgrown, infected, abandoned; in *Nostalgia* it is marginalised, theorised, while in *The Sacrifice* it is flat and cold – still beautiful in parts, but no longer vital. This changing natural landscape profoundly reflects Tarkovsky's own artistic and personal path.

Mirror had a long gestation period: ten years. It went through many stages and shapes, constantly being reworked, rethought, 're-remembered'. Its editing was a traumatic experience for Tarkovsky who watched it fall apart twenty times, before it finally 'gelled'. As ever, its course was riddled with ill will, interference from the authorities, scathing criticism and calculated indifference. And the director's own personal life was changing. He had finally dissolved his first marriage and had embarked on his second which, in the view of many people close to him, was to prove fatal for Tarkovsky the human being. In a certain sense he was saying goodbye to his past, to a whole period of his creative and personal life, and felt bound to reassess his direction. This was his mid-life crisis, voiced poetically in the film through the character of Liza, who quotes the opening lines of Dante's *Inferno*: 'Halfway through my earthly life, I lost my way in a gloomy forest.' *Mirror* was Tarkovsky's attempt to find his way out of the forest; it was a gathering place of all the tensions and realisations that beset him. It was also a leave-taking – of roots, of childhood, and of family and the family home in their broader sense. Old friends and collaborators fell away, to be replaced by new ones whose presence was also to be short-lived. Significantly, *Mirror* was the first film in which Tarkovsky broke ranks with his long-time collaborator and friend, the cinematographer Vadim Iusov. Georgi Rerberg, who replaced him, was fired in the early days of *Stalker*. Tarkovsky's last two films were made in Western Europe, in conditions he found difficult and alienating, with crews he did not know personally, with tight budgets and daunting time-schedules. And because, as he always maintained, his films *were* his life, and not career moves, all the changes and losses left an imprint on his spirit, which gradually became bereft of everything his camera had eulogised in *Mirror*.

Tarkovsky was convinced that a film built in its entirety on personal experience would become important for those who saw it. In March

1973, during the preparation for the shooting of *Mirror*, he wrote in his diary:

> Something has been happening to me recently ... I have started to feel that the time has come when I am ready to make the most important work of my life.
>
> The guarantee that this is so is, first, my own certainty ... and second, the material which I am going to use – which is simple, but at the same time extraordinarily profound; familiar and banal – to the point where one will not be distracted, not drawn away from what matters.
>
> I would even call it ideal material, because I feel and know it so well, I'm so aware of it. The only question is – shall I be able to do it? Shall I be able to imbue the perfectly constructed body with a soul?[1]

Evidence that he did so was the extraordinary response the film received. People of all backgrounds who saw the film sent him countless letters – ecstatic, confessional and grateful for his art. For the first time in his life, Tarkovsky had irrefutable proof that he had not been creating in a void, for an elite audience – a constant accusation – but for an audience that had a deep need of his work. Not all the letters were complimentary; some of those writing were hostile, others were baffled and confused. The sympathetic ones spoke of the film as an event, as an act, as a direct conversation with the viewer, as an awakening. And the refrain, echoing through all the letters, was 'this is a film about me'.

I saw *Mirror* in my native Athens, in the early 1980s. At the time I knew nothing of Russian language, culture or history and had no context with which to understand the deeper significance of some of the episodes in the film. Yet I, too, instinctively felt that this was a film about me. In fact, it was more than a film; it was a reality that I could inhabit. The emotions I experienced are best expressed by two of the letters in Tarkovsky's archives. A woman from Novosibirsk wrote:

> Everything that torments me, everything I lack and that I long for, that makes me indignant, and sick, and that suffocates me, everything

that gives me light and warmth and by which I live, and everything that destroys me – I saw it all in your film, as if inside a mirror.
For the first time ever, a film has become a reality for me, and that
is why I go to see it, to get inside it, to *live* there.

And a woman from Gorky summed it up like this: 'in that dark hall,
looking at a piece of canvas lit up by your talent, I felt for the first
time in my life that I was not alone.'[2] It is rare that a film can
provoke such reactions. Most of us still visit the cinema for entertain-
ment, or escapism, not for spiritual sustenance, for revelations and
benedictions. Yet those of us who are 'Tarkovsky-marked' experience
his films in just such religious terms. Analysis is not usually conducive
to this type of experience, yet through it one hopes to unravel something of the mysterious and ineffable process of creation. Tarkovsky
distrusted analysis, believing that a work of art is more than the sum
of its parts. He asked people to look at his films the way they would
look at the passing landscape through a train window. *Mirror* is a vast
Russian landscape, yielding something new with each visit. Like all
true works of art, it is inexhaustible.

The Film's Form

If we were to oversimplify, we might conclude that *Mirror* is a film
about a dying man who reflects on the essential moments of his life.
But *Mirror* has a richness and complexity that encompasses more
than the memories and reflections of a single life. It is a plotless film,
constructed like a vast mosaic, each piece of which represents a
unique experience or event in the life of the protagonists, in the life
of the country, and in the history of the world. Some of the events
are real, employing documentary footage; others are reconstructed
from memory; still others are invented and imagined. Past, present
and future are interwoven, as are reality, memory and dream. The
film has its own internal logic, which is that of a dream. Linear
sequentiality, character and plot motivation and development have
no place here. And it is not always clear whether it is Tarkovsky or
his characters who are doing the dreaming. The director appears to
prefer it that way, further obscuring the boundaries by using the same
actors to represent different people: Margarita Terekhova is both the

narrator's mother, Maria, and his estranged wife, Natalia; Ignat Daniltsev is both the narrator's son, Ignat, and the narrator himself as an adolescent.

The film's uniting consciousness is the narrator, Alexei, Tarkovsky's alter ego. He recounts to us his memories of childhood, the images and emotions that haunt and besiege him. We witness sequences from his childhood in the 1930s and 1940s, from his mother's life in those years and from his own life in the present. Interspersed with these is documentary footage of historical events, both national and international. There is also a series of episodes, which are part dream, part vision and part memory. These are filmed mostly in black and white or monochrome, though there is no strict colour coding to help the viewer find his way between the different layers of time and memory. Certain colour sequences constitute memories of the past, while others represent the present. Likewise, some dreams are filmed in colour, others in black and white. Another important off-screen presence, mirroring that of the narrator, is the poet Arseni Tarkovsky, Andrei Tarkovsky's father, who recites four of his poems at critical moments in the film.

There are three main time zones in the film: pre-war, war-time and post-war. The extended opening sequence (after the credits) takes place in and around the dacha the narrator spent some of his pre-war summers in, which he refers to as 'my grandfather's house' and 'the house of my childhood'. We are taken back to this house and the surrounding countryside several times in the film. Within that realm only the first scene – between Maria, the protagonist's mother, and a country doctor – is acted out as though in present time; the rest are filmed as dreams and visions, and are variously accompanied by silence, voice-over, poetry and sound effects. The long printing-works sequence also belongs to the pre-war period, unfolding during Stalin's Terror. The film concludes with the idyllic, pre-war landscape surrounding the dacha, where parents, children and grandmother are interwoven in an extraordinary illustration of the simultaneity of time.

There are three war-time sequences: one at the shooting range, the father's brief return from the war, and the attempted sale of earrings to a rich doctor's wife. Post-war sequences include those between Alexei, Natalia his ex-wife, and Ignat their son; a telephone call between Alexei and his mother, early in the film; and an episode with Spaniards, all of which take place in Alexei's flat. In this same post-war flat we also witness two strange women who appear to Ignat, an image of the past in the present, and Alexei on his deathbed, surrounded by his doctor and the two women. The film's documentary footage is mainly post-war, though the crossing of the Sivash river and the atomic bomb exploding in Hiroshima constitute some of the most harrowing and breathtaking images of war-time.

The film's prologue, the healing of the stutterer, also takes place in the present. This documentary sequence, filmed by Tarkovsky, introduces the film's entire fabric and pitch, as will be discussed later.

A Sequence-by-sequence Account

Present. Ignat turns on the television. We see a session between a woman speech therapist and a stutterer. The woman proceeds to heal the boy's stutter and admonishes him to speak 'loudly and clearly, freely and lightly'. He responds, 'I can speak'. *Credits*

Pre-war. Maria sits on a fence, in front of a wooden house, looking across a field. A man approaches her, asking for directions, and a conversation ensues. When he leaves, the camera follows her as she walks about the house, accompanied by the first poem *First Meetings*. We see her children, a boy and a girl, several other people and various objects and spaces in and around the house. The shed burns in the yard, with everyone looking silently on. *First dream*: The boy Alexei sleeps. We see the edge of the forest, and a gust of strong wind rushing towards us from within it. Alexei calls out 'Papa' and gets up. In the next room, the father rinses the mother's hair. She is dressed in white, her hair dripping. Rain and pieces of ceiling begin to fall inside the room. She walks towards a mirror, out of which an old woman (her future self) emerges. A hand shields a burning branch.

Present. In the narrator, Alexei's, flat we hear a telephone conversation between him and his mother, who tells him that her colleague from the printing works, Liza, has died.

Pre-war. Maria rushes to the printing works to check some proofs, fearing she has made a mistake. After checking the proofs, she returns to her department, accompanied by the poem *From morning on I waited yesterday.* Back at her desk, relieved, she whispers her imagined mistake to her friend Liza. Liza attacks her, comparing her to Maria Lebiadkina, a character from Dostoevsky's novel *The Devils*, and criticises her behaviour towards her husband and children. A male colleague witnesses the scene. Maria, tearful, goes to take a shower and recalls the fire at the dacha.

Present. At his flat, Alexei tells his estranged wife, Natalia, that he always believed she looked like his mother.

Pre-war. At the dacha, we see Maria and a dark-haired woman. We hear Alexei's voice saying how he always remembers his mother with Natalia's face.

Present. Natalia and Alexei bicker. He urges her to remarry so that Ignat does not turn out like him. She asks him to make up with his mother, but he says he can do nothing to stop them drifting apart. Ignat listens. In another room, a man is speaking in Spanish, excitedly, mimicking a matador. We see documentary footage of a bullfight. One of the other Spaniards present explains that the man is remembering life in Spain. We see footage of the Spanish Civil War, interspersed with the goings-on in the room. Then there is footage of Soviet stratosphere balloons and Soviet aviator Valeri Chkalov's triumphant return to Moscow, after flying across the North Pole. Ignat turns the pages of a book of Leonardo's drawings. Natalia leaves in a rush. Alone in the flat, Ignat is startled to find two women in one of the rooms. One of them asks him to read a letter from Pushkin to Chaadaev (see p. 61). The door bell rings and he opens it to his grandmother; they do not recognise each other and she moves on. When he returns to the room, the two women have disappeared. His father phones, asks him if he is in love, and tells him that at his age he was in love with a red-head, with whom his military instructor was also in love.

War-time. The red-head walks across a snowy landscape. The adolescent Alexei watches her. At the firing range, the military instructor gives a command, incorrectly executed by Asafiev. The instructor threatens to send him back to his parents, but is told he is an orphan, from the siege of Leningrad. Asafiev throws a dummy grenade, which the instructor, in a moment of panic, takes for real. We see footage of men crossing the Sivash lagoon in the Crimea, carrying a cannon. It is interspersed with a tearful Asafiev walking away. The sequence is accompanied by the poem *Life, Life*. Sequences of war-time and post-war footage are interspersed with shots of Asafiev at the top of the hill, where a bird comes to rest on his head. We see Maria cutting wood, when the father, in soldier's uniform, appears. His children fall into his arms, leaving behind them the same Leonardo volume Ignat had been looking at in a previous scene. We see a close-up of Leonardo's portrait of Ginevra de Benci.

Present. Natalia asks Alexei to visit more often because Ignat misses him. He asks her to let Ignat live with him. When Ignat is asked he declines. Natalia speaks to Alexei about his mother, about his feelings of guilt towards her, and her need to protect him as if he were still a child. Alexei is ironic about a writer Natalia is seeing, calling him Dostoevsky. Outside in the yard, Ignat has lit a fire. They argue over him again.

Pre-war. Second dream: The wind comes out of the forest, then the dacha and its occupants are seen. The narrator speaks about the dream, which compels him to return to the house where he was born. We see Maria, the boy Alexei, and the house, surrounded by trees. The wind knocks things off a wooden table.

War-time. Maria has gone to sell her earrings to Nadezhda Petrovna, a rich doctor's wife, taking the adolescent Alexei with her. While the women speak, he is left alone in the room, looking at his reflection in the mirror. He remembers the red-head, holding the burning branch. The doctor's wife shows Maria her baby son, lying in an opulent, lace-clad bed. Maria leaves the room abruptly, as if disgusted. The woman asks her to kill a chicken, which Maria initially refuses to do, but then concedes. She has a vision of her husband stroking her hand and herself levitating. She leaves the doctor's house hurriedly, taking the earrings, accompanied by the final poem, *Eyrydice*.

Pre-war. Third dream: The wind comes out of the forest, knocking things off the table. The boy Alexei runs into a room with hanging curtains, holding a jar with milk in front of a mirror. Then we see him swimming in a pond. Maria washes clothes by the river. We see the dacha, Maria, the old woman, the young Alexei and his sister.

Present. In Alexei's flat, a doctor is talking to the two women Ignat had met earlier, about Alexei's illness. Alexei, lying behind a door, asks to be left alone, saying he only wanted to be happy. His hand releases a bird up in the air.

2. The old mother (Maria Tarkovskaia) with her young children during the filming of the final sequence of *Mirror*, Ignatievo, summer 1973. (Photograph: Vladimir Murashko)

Pre-war. We see the landscape around the dacha and Maria and her husband lying in a field. He asks her if she wants a girl or a boy. We see the old mother, with the two young children, and follow her as she walks through the shrubs with the children, while the young Maria watches them from a distance. The camera follows them until they walk out of its range, and then retreats into the forest.

Notes

1. A. Tarkovsky, *Time within Time. The Diaries* (Calcutta, 1991), p. 74.
2. O. Surkova, *Kniga sopostavlenii* (Moscow, 1991), p. 176.

2. *Mirror*: A Production History

'We, of course, have freedom of speech here. But not to such an extent!'[1]

The Beginning, 1964

Tarkovsky's journey towards *Mirror* was one involving both his heart-felt human emotions and his formal concerns in the medium of film. It is a journey he has described, in part, and with variations, in his lectures, writings and interviews. His earliest written reference to it is in a long article, first published in 1964, in which he discussed the experience of making *Ivan's Childhood* and put forth some of his thoughts on cinema.[2] In this article, he explicitly revealed his interest in creating a personal world of memories through the medium of film. He spoke of the preciousness of our memories, suggesting that the most beautiful ones are those of childhood. He stressed, however, that memories must undergo a special process before they can be worked into an artistic reconstruction of the past. He felt that by using the properties of memory one could develop a working principle on which to base a compelling film. Instead of following an external logic of events, and the actions and behaviour of the central hero, the film would show his thoughts, recollections and dreams; it would reveal his inner world, while he himself remained outside the film frame. This would put him on a par with the lyric hero of poetry – absent from view but permeating the work with his sensibility. Tarkovsky also declared his preference for the logic of poetry over conventional plot and character development, believing that poetic links are closer to the laws by which thought – and life itself – evolves, and should therefore dictate the sequence of events and the editing of a film. He suggested that this approach stimulates the viewer, because it does not impose upon him a final conclusion; instead, it makes him a participant in what is unfolding on screen – heightening his emotional response, prompting him to make his own associative links, making him into a co-creator.

In 1964, Tarkovsky was also working on a script based on the life of the fourteenth-century Russian icon painter, Andrei Rublev, together with his friend and fellow director, Andrei Konchalovsky. In his memoirs, Konchalovsky writes that one day he returned home after an absence of four hours (Tarkovsky was staying with him at the time), to find an almost empty bottle of vodka and several typed pages by the typewriter. Tarkovsky had written down some childhood recollections of his mother, and a story about a shell-shocked military instructor. To Konchalovsky these pages were pure literature – nothing in them remotely resembled a film script.[3] Indeed, as Tarkovsky writes in *Sculpting in Time*, his initial idea was to put down on paper 'the memories that plagued me; at that point I had no thought of a film. It was to be a novella about the war-time evacuation, and the plot was to be centred on the military instructor at my school.'[4] Many years later, when Tarkovsky was lecturing on film directing at the Advanced Courses for Scriptwriters and Directors in Moscow, this is how he described to his students the circumstances surrounding the making of *Mirror*:

> I only know that I kept dreaming the same dream about the house where I was born. I dreamed of the house. And then as if I was walking into it, or rather, not into it but around it all the time. These dreams were terribly real, although I knew even then that I was only dreaming. And it was always the same dream, because it took part in the same place. I believed that this feeling carried some material sense, something very important, for why should such a dream pursue a man so?[5]

With his awareness of Freud and love of Proust, Tarkovsky decided that if he found a way to speak of these emotions he would be set free. The story that Konchalovsky stumbled upon was the initial

expression of his emotions, which Tarkovsky called *A White Day.*
The title was inspired by a poem his father had written in 1942
beginning:

> A stone lies by the jasmine,
> Under the stone, a treasure,
> Father stands on the road,
> A white, white day.

The poem speaks of childhood happiness and the impossibility of
ever returning to it. The abiding sense of nostalgia, beauty and loss
evoked by it became one of the underlying themes of *Mirror.* The
poem also lent its title – *A White, White Day* – to the early versions
of the script.

As an epigraph to his own *White Day,* Tarkovsky used the first
verse of another of his father's poems, called *Song,* written in 1960:

> My early years have long since passed,
> Along the very edge,
> Along the very edge of my native land,
> Along the sloping mint, along the dark blue heaven,
> This heaven I am losing forever.
>
> On the opposite shore, the willow sways,
> Like white arms.
> I cannot walk along the bridge to the end,
> But I carry in my memory the moist sounds,
> Of that finest name, on our final parting.
>
> She stands by the curve,
> And washes her white arms in the water,
> And I bear her an eternal debt.
> If only I could say who it is that stands on the water-meadow,
> On the opposite shore,
> By the willow tree, like a mermaid by the river,
> Casting her ring from finger to finger.

The woman in this poem, to whom the writer bears an eternal debt,
is, in Tarkovsky's consciousness, his own mother. In *Mirror* he re-
creates this white-armed, willow-like woman, in the first dream, that
of the 'weeping room' where the mother has been washing her hair.

The film internalises the images of the father and the woman/mother from the two poems, paying homage to this shimmering, fragile Eden of childhood and love, which invariably dies. The poems' presence reveals that one of the earliest pieces of the puzzle that became *Mirror* was Arseni Tarkovsky's creative consciousness and poetic voice. This silent dialogue between father and son is one of the essential components of the film, and is revealed in some of the most powerful couplings between word and image in the director's work.

Story, Proposal and Script, 1967–68

A White Day, which Tarkovsky decided to publish in 1970, includes an elaborate version of the film's earring episode, and an account of the destruction of the cupolas of the Simonov church in the village of Iurievets, on the Volga – Tarkovsky had witnessed this while living there during the war years – a sequence which is present in most versions of the script, but which was dropped before filming. Tarkovsky had excised the episode with the military instructor. The story also contains an interesting self-analysis by Sergei, the narrator, a thinly veiled version of Tarkovsky:

> I was cunning and observant. My cunning fed my powers of observation, and together with my inability to hide it, it crystallised into a loathsome and painful defencelessness. This defencelessness found its peculiar expression in my pathological unwillingness to act when needed. I totally hardened in my pleasurable empirical zeal. I resembled a plant, a gourd, whose practical intent in releasing its curling tendrils is to find something to grab on to. The trouble is I found nothing to grab on to. The gourd was abnormal [...] Its tendrils did not rush to a support, they shuddered in the green, warm darkness of the garden herbs instead, with a futile intensity, but bereft of purpose.[6]

This revealing self-portrait is corroborated by Tarkovsky's sister, Marina Tarkovskaia, who has spoken of his unfocused energy in his childhood and youth, and the great pain it gave their mother, Maria Vishniakova. Tarkovsky entered VGIK [the All Union State Institute of Cinematography] in Moscow in 1954, at the suggestion of a friend of his father's who had acquaintances there and offered to help the Tarkovskys with their troublesome, confused son.

The project that was to become *Mirror* closely resembled the 'abnormal' gourd Tarkovsky once believed himself to be. It was growing with intensity, but without a clear and secure framework to relate to. The original proposal,[7] *Confession*, submitted to the Mosfilm studio at the end of 1967, is evidence of this; and although Tarkovsky always professed an aversion to experiments in film, it is hard to ignore the experimental nature of the film he puts forward. Tarkovsky called it a 'film-survey' [fil'm-anketa], which would be built piecemeal around an extended interview with a mother about her life; through her he intended to illustrate aspects of the country's culture and history, and differences between the generations, by introducing the woman's son. Based on the mother's responses, he would 'reconstruct' episodes from her life and from her son's life. The film itself would begin to emerge on the editing table, after all the material had been shot. Tarkovsky stated that he wanted the film to be like a literary creation, whereby the work achieves its final form only at the very end. A contract for the development of a literary script was drawn up on 9 January 1968.

It is surprising that the go-ahead for a script based on such a convoluted and vague proposal was given at all. It must be remembered that in the Soviet period film proposals were elaborate games of hide-and-seek with those who took the decisions on what was worthy and unworthy of being produced. Here ideology, rather than financial profit, was the issue. Some of Tarkovsky's intent, therefore, had to remain hidden in order for him to be allowed through to the next stage: the writing of a literary script.[8] Tarkovsky's high moral tone, his pronouncements on key Soviet themes such as the Mother, the Second World War, one's duty to country and kin, were all deliberate, in order to satisfy ideology and bypass the censor. The fact remains, however, that he was uncertain of the outcome of the proposed film and not altogether clear about the means he intended to employ in order to achieve his ambitious project. A closer examination of the film's production and editing history will reveal that Tarkovsky often moved blindly, feeling his way, one step at a time, relying largely on intuition and instinct.

Tarkovsky co-authored the script with his friend, the playwright Alexander Misharin. In his memoir of the director, Misharin gave a detailed account of their collaboration.[9] At the beginning of 1968, the two men went to the cinematographers' retreat in Repino to write the script. They spent the first month relaxing, meeting friends, doing everything but working. Then, towards the end of February, when most people had left, they sat down to work. First they talked about events from their own lives, things recounted by others, or read in books. These discussions led to the formation of episodes, the contents of which, Misharin notes with amazement, Tarkovsky was never vague about. He knew from the outset what they would look like, what images they would encompass, how they would be resolved, down to the last detail, even the last phrase. They committed nothing to paper – everything was retained in their memory at this stage. Finally they ended up with thirty-six episodes, which they managed to pare down to the twenty-eight that would eventually go into the script. 'With the lightness of genius and the rashness of youth', as Misharin put it, they estimated it would take them fourteen days to write everything out. Every day they decided who would tackle which episode, then went away, each to his own room, to write, and met again at five in the afternoon to read the finished product to each other. They vowed never to reveal who had written which episode, and Misharin was offended when Tarkovsky subsequently published *A White Day*, although he had conceived it years before the existence of the script.

Several versions of the literary script are held at the Mosfilm archives,[10] which contain a wealth of material on films. A film's every stage, from the earliest proposal to the final edit, was discussed in minute detail, first by a script board, at the script level, then by an artistic council at the filming stage. The central government body for cinema, Goskino, had to give its approval before the project could move on to the next stage. All aspects of production were recorded and transcribed where necessary, photocopied and kept on file. The most revealing documents are the transcriptions of the discussions that took place during the development of script and film. The boards consisted of an array of editors, directors, and cameramen, actors, scriptwriters and bureaucrats, all of whom expressed their opinions on the material under discussion. Tarkovsky loathed these sessions, and was often driven to anger and despair at having to defend and explain himself to people he considered below him in terms of culture, talent and dedication. Indeed, there were instances of extreme philistinism and crassness. But the councils also included talented film-makers, who took a genuine interest in Tarkovsky's work. And, although he never admitted as much, their suggestions and remarks did have a bearing on his films. Their comments and readings – even their doubts – served to foreground, clarify and refine areas that might have otherwise remained problematic. Tarkovsky often fought back, but these were also fruitful battles which helped him develop his ideas and his craft. Some of the best known among the film-makers, whose names appear regularly in the discussions, were the two-man team Alov and Naumov (who were also the artistic directors of the Fourth Creative Unit, where *Mirror* was shot), Marlen Khutsiev, director of one of the seminal films of the 1960s, *I am Twenty* [Mne dvatsat' let, 1965], and Mikhail Shveitser, director of *The Golden Calf* [Zolotoi telenok, 1968].

The Mosfilm documents on *Mirror* begin in 1968, with the proposal and the first version of the script. It is interesting to note that three of the central episodes of the film – the sequence in the printing works, the one with the military instructor, and the attempted earring sale – exist, in this earliest version, almost in their final form. Other, briefer sequences, such as the mother waiting for the father at the beginning of the film, the father's visit to the children while on furlough, as well as some of the narrator's childhood reminiscences, and his phone conversation with his mother, are also present. The early script's closing pages contain the essential images and emotions that we witness in the film's final sequences. All the other episodes were dropped when it came to filming.

The one notable presence in every version of the script is a long questionnaire of over 200 questions intended for Tarkovsky's mother. These range from asking about her favourite colour, animal and tree, to questions about art, flying saucers, nuclear energy and civic duty. There are many war-time episodes, which reveal the narrator's anger and shame over the deprivations that he suffered as a child in those years. The narrator's voice is far more present in the script – he ruminates on death and loss prompted by a sequence at a cemetery, he reflects on art, on his childhood, his mother, lost hopes and lost freedom. There is a long sequence at the hippodrome, involving the narrator, his mother and sister. There are also two intriguing hallucinatory scenes. One involves the narrator swimming underwater, among the submerged village of Zavrazhe, where he was born (see p. 71); in the other he looks at his reflection in a mirror to find there a young face staring back at him, while his own face is on someone else, calmly leaning against a wall in the same room.[11] In the early script Tarkovsky included several passages from Leonardo's description of how to paint a battle scene. He wanted to include this scene in order to give a broader historical backdrop to the lives of the characters, but the studio bureaucrats considered it irrelevant and asked for it to be cut. In the film it was replaced with the war footage, and the Pushkin letter read by Ignat to the two women, while the Leonardo extracts gave way to the thick book of his drawings, and the portrait of Ginevra de Benci. The narrator's imminent death at the end of the film is a thematic transformation of the script's opening sequence – his thoughts on death, on a snowy winter's day at someone's funeral.

The minutes of a studio discussion of the first version of the script in April 1968 foreground several problem areas. There was concern over the questions: some people felt they were too many and too chaotic, others wanted to know exactly how they would be filmed. Tarkovsky explained that his own mother would be the interviewee, and that the questions would be asked by a woman psychiatrist, posing as a member of the crew who was conducting research on the film he was making. Their meetings – which were to take the form of a conversation, rather than an interview – would be filmed with a hidden camera, for he did not want his mother to know that she was the main character in his film. Tarkovsky said that he was not interested in *what* his mother would reply to the questions, but in how she would respond; avoiding a question would be more revealing of her character than giving an answer. He explained:

> I cannot come to terms with the fact that my mother will die, I cannot agree with this. I will protest and show that my mother is immortal. I want to convince others of her striking individuality, of her uniqueness. The internal premise is to analyse her character with the claim that she is immortal. I want to pose the question 'why is she immortal?'[12]

Some of those present, however, felt that the boy – the author in his youth – took up a disproportionately large part of the script, pushing the mother into the background. They pointed out that the mother came across as flat and monotonous in the fictional episodes, when she should respond with more passion and extroversion. Another criticism was that the script concentrated on intimate things, and lost the sense of range and immensity that was promised in the proposal, where the authors spoke of placing the mother in the context of her time. Yet others took issue with the relationship between the mother and her son, saying it was too flat, when there should be 'internal cataclysms between them'. Tarkovsky reacted strongly to this, replying that there would be no cataclysms whatsoever because this would kill his intention; he assured them that the monotony he was accused of was the most important and valuable thing for him, because he wanted to show his mother as *he* remembered her. What to his colleagues seemed monotonous, however, was for the director the sublimation of emotion into an 'Olympian calm of form' (see 'Tarkovsky's Cinematic Language', p. 47), and he knew well that giving his mother a more conventional response to her misfortunes and difficulties would kill his image of her spirit and stoicism. The only criticism he took on board was the episode of the death of the shell-shocked instructor (in this version the instructor throws himself on to a real grenade, which explodes and kills him). This was viewed as trite – even though it was based on a real event – because it was a subject often treated in works of literature. The meeting closed with a decision to treat the script as a first version, and ask its authors to write a second version, taking into account the recommendations of the artistic council.

A letter dated 18 November 1968 reveals that, although the authors did cut some of the interview questions, they made no significant changes to the character of the mother, nor did they attempt to show her in the context of her time. The script board decided to suspend all further work on the project – which it still considered 'exceptionally interesting' – unless the authors incorporated their recommendations in any future versions of the script. The rejection appeared to have come from the then head of Goskino, Alexei Romanov. Tarkovsky took the rejection with uncharacteristic meekness, not even attempting to rework the script. Instead, he went on to make *Solaris*, alienating Misharin, who stopped talking to him for several years. It has to be remembered, however, that Tarkovsky had come out of a long battle on behalf of *Andrei Rublev* which, after having been hailed as a masterpiece, was shelved indefinitely in 1967. He was not the only one to suffer; a wave of films were relegated to the shelf in the years 1967–68, and many more proposals were rejected in what amounted to a pogrom that swept through Soviet cinema. Nor was Tarkovsky aided by the very nature of his project – a film with no strict boundaries, with no definitive shooting script, which he intended to put together, piecemeal, during the shooting.

A Second Beginning, 1970–73

Tarkovsky's thoughts, however, were never far from his aborted project. From the very first page of his published diary, which began in April 1970, he mentioned *A White Day* (translated as *The Bright Day* in the diary), saying it was the film he wanted to make as soon as he completed *Solaris*. In June he met the Swedish actress Bibi Andersson, and immediately decided she would be wonderful as the mother. In September he wrote in his diary:

> What will our children be like? A lot depends on us. But it's up to them as well. What must be alive in them is a striving for freedom. That depends on us. People who have been born into slavery find it hard to lose the habit. On the one hand it would be good if the next generation could enjoy some measure of peace; on the other hand peace can be a dangerous thing. Philistinism and all that is petty bourgeois in us inclines heavily towards peace. Whatever happens, they mustn't slide into spiritual lethargy. The most important things to instil in children are virtue and a sense of honour. Whatever happens I must make *The Bright Day*. That is part of the same work. A duty [...] I think constantly about *The Bright Day*. It could make a beautiful picture. It will actually be an instance of a film built in its entirety on personal experience. And for that reason, I am convinced, it will be important for those who see it.[13]

On 18 September 1970 he wrote that Grigori Chukhrai, the director of the experimental unit at Mosfilm, had asked to read the script of *A White Day*. Tarkovsky voiced his distrust of Chukhrai, and considered waiting to see whether Sergei Bondarchuk, the successful and influential director, would set up his own creative unit at Mosfilm. Bondarchuk had invited Tarkovsky to join it, and he preferred to make the film with him.

The beginning of 1971 saw Tarkovsky also becoming more involved with a script entitled *Light Wind* based on the science-fiction story *Ariel* by the popular children's writer, Alexander Beliaev.[14] But *A White Day* was never far from his thoughts. In August he was discussing the project with Chukhrai again, deciding on the length of the film, which Chukhrai thought should not be more than 3100 m (112 minutes). Tarkovsky wanted to press for more footage because the script was long, but eventually agreed with him, and estimated he would begin writing the shooting script in August of the following year. He also decided to add the battle of Kulikovo[15] to *A White Day*. He wanted to film this parallel to the sequence of the destruction of the Simonov church, though when he finally included this sequence he juxtaposed it with Leonardo's description of how to paint a battle scene.

In early 1972, Tarkovsky began having doubts about his long-time cinematographer, Vadim Iusov: 'The film will be difficult; I will have to "strip naked" and Vadim is not close enough to me, nor spiritually rich enough (I am not even sure he has a soul) for me to trust in him. At one level he is a pleb. Should I invite Rerberg to work on the film?'[16] Tarkovsky was still unsure whether *A White Day* or *Light Wind* would be the next film he would make, but decided to go ahead with whichever script the studio accepted. He gave the director of Mosfilm, Nikolai Sizov, both scripts, but Sizov disliked both, saying that they wanted him to make a topical and relevant film. Tarkovsky protested that his work was about maintaining the standard of Soviet cinema, not the relevant or the topical. Some time later he was told that *A White Day* would go through provided he gave a detailed explanation of the idea of the film, which was deemed unclear. Ironically, the man responsible for this decision was the new head of Goskino, Filipp Ermash, whom Tarkovsky in later years came to view as his nemesis. In those early days, Ermash dreamed of a renaissance of Soviet film, which he would initiate and preside over. He let Elem Klimov start work on a twice-rejected script, *Agony* [Agoniia, 1975]. He gave the go-ahead for Vasili Shukshin's *Red Berry* [Kalina krasnaia, 1974] and Andrei Smirnov's *Autumn* [Osen', 1975].

To Tarkovsky he said: 'You can film whatever you want.' Tarkovsky submitted two proposals: *Confession* and *Light Wind*. The former was accepted. But, according to Misharin, Tarkovsky stalled, wary of the fact that he would be exposing himself through the film, and unclear of how he would resolve the problem of filming the interview with his mother. A series of intense discussions ensued, but the solution came in the most unexpected way. One day Misharin gave Tarkovsky the Soviet writer Vasili Grossman's last novel, *Everything Flows*, and asked him to read one particular chapter – about a drug addict's wife who goes through all the circles of hell – out loud. Tarkovsky read through it in tears; when he had finished, he had also crossed the Rubicon and was free to begin.

On 17 September 1972, a meeting took place between Tarkovsky, Sizov, Naumov, Ermash, and his deputy, Baskakov, in Ermash's office. Tarkovsky explained how he saw the film, speaking purposely about the connection between the characters and the country, the life of the country 'and all that'. They all wanted him to make a film about scientific and technical progress, but he told them that he was interested in humanitarian questions. He was again asked to write down in detail the idea of the future film and to indicate the changes he would make to the shooting script, as opposed to the literary script. It was agreed that once they had read what he had to say – provided it was satisfactory – he could start work on the shooting script which, however, would have to be shortened to 3200 m (115 minutes). In December, Tarkovsky wrote in his diary that he was about to get the go-ahead for *A White Day*, but that Iusov had declined to work on it with him. Tarkovsky believed he did this on purpose, when he was most needed, in order to cause the greatest possible distress. He was convinced that Iusov had never really liked him, and never agreed with the concept of the film: 'In his lower-middle-class way he was infuriated by the fact that I was making a film about myself.'[17]

The Mosfilm archive becomes active again in September 1972 with the first discussion of the old script taking place on 18 October. Tarkovsky intended to add some documentary footage and two new episodes. One involved a group of Spaniards at a café, reminiscing about their lives in Spain before they boarded the Soviet ships that brought them to the port of Odessa; they were child refugees, fleeing the Spanish Civil War. The other was the battle of Kulikovo. The end of that year sees a satisfied letter from the various directors of the Fourth Creative Unit, on the changes and successful additions made to the script. What was interpreted as a shift in accent and meaning in the episodes of the shell-shocked instructor (the grenade here becomes a dummy) and the printing works was seen as a welcome change, as was the omission of the episode of the destruction of the Simonov church.

In early 1973, and while waiting to hear whether his revised script of *A White Day* had been accepted, Tarkovsky reflected on the medium of film, in a way that was to have a direct bearing on *Mirror*:

> One has to work out a principle, which allows for film to affect people individually. The 'total' image must become something private, comparable with the images of literature, painting, poetry, music. The basic principle – as it were, the mainspring – is, I think, that as little as possible has actually to be shown, and from that little the audience has to build up an idea of the rest, of the whole. In my view that has to be the basis for constructing the cinematographic image. And if one looks at it from the point of view of symbols, then the symbol in cinema is a symbol of nature, of reality. Of course it isn't a question of details, but of what is hidden.[18]

Tarkovsky wanted desperately to work, but time was passing, and the studio remained noncommittal. Still, he pondered the title of the film, deciding that *A White Day* was too weak and flat (see 'Author and Hero', p. 80). Meanwhile, he met with his new cameraman, Georgi Rerberg, to discuss the film. He reported that Rerberg felt they were treating the material in a traditional way that was not original enough. But Tarkovsky believed Rerberg wrong: 'We must strive for simplicity. Everything must be simple and profound. The simpler, the more profound. Everything must be simple, free, natural, without false tension. That is the ideal.'[19] Yet he enjoyed working with Rerberg, admitting he had never worked so easily and enjoyably with anyone else.

Two months later, in February 1973, the studio received a letter from Goskino, asking the authors to review some of the tactless questions to the mother, and to develop the new episodes of the Spaniards and the battle of Kulikovo, in order to show a more optimistic, patriotic and heroic outlook. On 23 March 1973, Tarkovsky wrote in his diary that he felt 'the time has come when I am ready to make the most important work of my life' (see Chapter 1, p. 3). While his wife, Larisa, together with other members of the crew, travelled to Leningrad, Pskov and Novgorod to look for actors, Tarkovsky reflected on the fate of the cinema, on how it had degenerated into something wholly insignificant. He wanted his film to be tantamount to an act, a deed, for which he anticipated being crucified by the powers that be, since he was sure they would feel insulted. At this time, Tarkovsky began to keep a workbook on the film. He kept workbooks on all his films, but the two thick A5 diaries on *Mirror* are by far the most elaborate and detailed of all of them. They contain literary quotations, fragments of dialogue, the day's shooting schedule, changes to script and shots, thoughts on music and soundtrack, and most of the painful twenty-one edits Tarkovsky attempted before the film finally came together in the form in which we know it today. Tarkovsky also recorded meetings with the authorities, angry exchanges, his frustration with people and events, and pasted in photographs of actors and crew on set, as well as outtakes from the film – notably one of himself as the dying author at the end, holding a small bird.

The first workbook begins on 22 March 1973 with several quotations from Thomas Mann's *Doctor Faustus*, which Tarkovsky had been reading with great relish at the time and which remained, for many years, one of the works he wanted to adapt for the screen. Leverkuhn was a character he felt he understood inherently; the artist's torment, his loneliness, his search for ultimate truth and the price he pays for achieving it, the battle between flesh and spirit, God and the devil – Tarkovsky inhabited these ideas and emotions throughout his short life. The passages he quotes are taken from the book's first two chapters and address questions of love and indifference, reflections on music, the constant, and necessary, presence of the powers of the underworld over the spheres of human endeavour and human culture, and the propitiatory communion between the dark forces and the Olympian Gods. Tarkovsky adds his own thoughts to those of Mann: 'I have always believed that, in the end, everything is equilibrated – or at least it strives towards equilibrium. Of course, it is not the same thing. That is why there can be no harmony without the demon.'[20] In the pages that follow he jots down his ideas about the form of the film, its mood and atmosphere, and what he wants to achieve: 'The film's organism must live independently of the author, in fact like any work of art'; 'Magritte, with his particular metaphysics and blurring of the borders between reality and fantasy is closer to the [film's] stylistics'; 'Amorous experiences – childhood'; 'Olympian calm'; 'Coldness. The price of coldness'; 'The temperament of Rublev the painter, Bach the musician. What is temperament?'

Mirror in Production, 1973–74

Mosfilm gave the go-ahead for the development of a shooting script on 26 March 1973; this, in essence, signified the beginning of production. In writing the shooting script, Tarkovsky attempted to create some consistency between the interview questions put to his mother and the fictional scenes that follow: the questions were organised around certain themes that were picked up by the fictional episodes. He also included some of the documentary footage he was later going to use in the film. This was partly a result of calls for more historical context from the studio bosses. All the episodes from the literary script are present, with a few variations and changes of accent.

A curiosity in the archive at this point is a letter, dated 17 April 1973, sent to Gosfilmofond [the State Film Archive] asking them to allow the crew of *A White Day* to view certain films in their collection. These, apparently, were to be of aid to the experimental and complex nature of the film they wanted to make. There follows a list of the films:

> *From Russia with Love*
> *Goldfinger*
> *The Good, the Bad and the Ugly*
> *For a Few Dollars More*
> *Once Upon a Time in the West*
> *Roma*
> *8 1/2*
> *Zéro de Conduite*

The relevance of the last three films is indisputable; but what can we

3. Tarkovsky on set in the winter of 1973, holding the clapper-board, which reads *A White White Day*. (Photograph: Vladimir Murashko)

make of the first five in the context of *Mirror*, except to surmise that members of the crew were loyal fans of special agent 007 and spaghetti westerns. The existence of such a whimsical official document is yet another reminder of the absurdity of the Soviet system, so critical and punitive and yet at times so surprisingly permissive.

The discussion that took place on 27 April 1973 over the newly written shooting script covered a lot of interesting ground, and brought up issues that changed the shape of the film. The interview questions constituted the main problem; people were worried that they would not flow smoothly with the fictional episodes, and that they would end up swamping the film. Their main concern was the prospect of filming Tarkovsky's mother with a hidden camera. Naumov believed that it was unethical to deceive her in this way, yet admitted that if she knew she was being filmed it would destroy the authenticity of her responses. The second important issue came up when Khutsiev asked who would act the author of the film, to which Tarkovsky responded 'I will'. Khutsiev protested that there is a difference between 'I' and 'Author' in a work of art, pointing out that in lyric poetry the 'I' encompasses more than the author of the verses, and that if one speaks as oneself, one can never say everything. Naumov felt that Tarkovsky's presence as the author would be tactless and immodest, that in fact the film's strength and its personal quality would be enhanced by excluding concrete people and preserving anonymity. Shveitser called attention to the script's confessional tone, adding that this was a first attempt at creating a confessional genre in film. He went on to say that, ideally, all art should be a confession, and that people need both to hear a confession and to confess. He urged Tarkovsky to combine the individual with the universal, because this would guarantee the film's success in terms of the audience's empathy with the author. Naumov pointed out that there was an excess of ideas on the verbal plane, which would be more effective if expressed in images and in the film's plastic realisation.

Tarkovsky reacted emotionally, as he always did, feeling attacked and misunderstood. He explained that everything would depend on how the interview turned out, since everything would be organised around that. He conceded that all would become clear in the editing stage, admitted to having more doubts than them, but added, 'there are things which I cannot explain right now, but which are very clear to me. I have an inner conviction that what I am attempting to do will succeed.'[21] He agreed with Shveitser that the relationship between author and public is very important, and explained that what is typical and universal, in his view, is to be found within the personal, the individual and the inimitable; that is where he can tap into people's empathy. He finished by saying that for him this film was an act, a way of being answerable for his actions.

The letter resulting from this discussion concluded that certain elements of the director's script must be reworked, and several episodes taken out altogether. These included a newly added sequence of the mother's trip to Rome, and the battle of Kulikovo, both of which, it was felt, did not fit organically within the context of the film. Doubts were raised about the episode at the hippodrome – both as a site and in terms of a newly added monologue about the author's guilt towards his mother. Tarkovsky was urged to use more historical footage, and to find organic ties between the different layers – interview, fictional and documentary – of the film, relying more on visual solutions than on philosophical text. Tarkovsky was also asked to make cuts, as the footage kept expanding (the initial agreed amount was 2700 m/98 minutes).

Tarkovsky continued to work on the shooting script, writing a new scene (the opening scene at the dacha) for Anatoli Solonitsyn, his favourite actor, and some of the author's monologues. The next few days were spent looking for locations: Tarkovsky looked at the Obraztsovo printing works, where his mother had once worked as a corrector, and went to Ignatievo, where he decided to rebuild his childhood house on the ruins of the original one (see 'Mirror's Chronotopes', p. 70). In his workbook, Tarkovsky made lists of documentary footage, the air-balloons and the atomic explosion already among them. He was still intending to go ahead with the interview of his mother, for which he looked for a suitable flat. At the end of May Tarkovsky composed an exasperated list of everything he did *not* have: no main actors, no flat for the interview and, more importantly, no official acceptance of the shooting script. By 1 June 1973, some of the important issues had been decided: the interview was to take place not with the mother, but with her friends and acquaintances, the author was not to appear on screen, and there was to be no battle of Kulikovo. Tarkovsky intensified his search for the main actress, finally choosing Margarita Terekhova late in June.

On 9 July, Tarkovsky wrote in his diary: 'At the dacha the buckwheat blossomed' (see 'Preparations for Filming *Mirror*', p. 42); this was the benign sign he had been waiting for. On 10 July he was told he could have 7500 m of Kodak film, which would allow for three takes per shot (in fact he was given less film, and mostly did one take per shot). Tarkovsky's mother arrived in Ignatievo on 19 July 1973, and shooting of the summer outdoor scenes officially began on the 21st. The first sequence shot was the film's opening scene between the mother and the stranger. Most of the scenes in and around the dacha were shot during this period, though it was a slow start, as is evidenced by an angry telegram sent by the studio, which reprimanded the director and crew for the miserly footage shot – 620 m (22 minutes) in over six weeks. The slowness was mostly due to Tarkovsky's constantly questioning the contents of the film. In his workbook he wrote:

> We're thinking of getting rid of the interview altogether; instead we want to film conversations about art – about the meaning of the artist, about the meaning of the actor who lives someone else's life through his character. About the fact that art is a search for absolute truth, which it perceives as an IMAGE of this truth, as its illusion. I don't believe in the interview! I will have to rewrite all of the author's monologues.

In September, when he returned to Moscow to view the rushes, Tarkovsky, according to his workbook, was dissatisfied with the results and decided to ask to be allowed to keep the sets on location in Ignatievo. In his diary, however, he wrote that he was happy with the

4. Tarkovsky with his mother on set in Ignatievo, summer 1973. (Photograph: Vladimir Murashko)

material shot, but that he had difficulty working with Rerberg, who was being rude to the crew. Filming was to resume on 2 November 1973 and end on 18 March 1974.

The first discussion on the material shot up to that point took place on 14 December 1973. Tarkovsky had spent the previous day editing together the printing-works episode, the childhood dreams, as well as scenes set in and around the dacha in Ignatievo, the earring episode, and the film's final sequence. He had also included some documentary footage, among which was the laborious crossing of the Sivash lagoon in the northern Crimea, part of the Soviet advance of 1943. He used his own voice in a rough recording of the narrator's text, and some of his father's poetry.

This first meeting went well. In his workbook and diary, Tarkovsky wrote that everyone was amazed at the material, while he himself felt confused by it and baffled by people's reactions. Everyone present spoke of the power and uniqueness of what they had seen; some people had even wept during the screening. Attention was called to a certain monotony in pace and rhythm, and to the long duration of the Sivash sequence – it was feared that it might induce laughter, rather than communicate a heroic feat. There was criticism of the child's room in the earring episode (it was deemed pompous and vulgar) and of the dreams not being interesting enough. The unit's artistic director, Boris Kremnev, said he was very moved by the people and events unfolding on screen, mentioned Tarkovsky's remarkable ability to communicate the life of the nation without having to resort to staple shots of factories and construction sites, and urged him to preserve the rough and fragmentary nature of the film during the editing period. Naumov, on the contrary, said he had a sense of a desert island, of a hermetically sealed inner world, while watching the film. He asked to see more of contemporary life and its pace, and expressed his misgivings over the dreams of childhood. Tarkovsky assured him that there would be a change of pace and that additional scenes would juxtapose contemporary life with the pre-war period. He explained that the dreams were an illustration of the author's recurring dream of returning to his childhood home. He also informed them 'gently', as he later wrote in his workbook, that he was thinking of replacing the interview with the mother – which he now felt might actually damage the film – with more fictional scenes. This pleased everyone, as the interview had been the most controversial aspect of the project. Everyone praised Terekhova's acting, suggesting that she should be used more, to which Tarkovsky happily responded that in fact they would also give her the role of a contemporary woman.

Tarkovsky spent the rest of December recording the soundtrack, waiting for the sets of the shooting range to be made ready for filming, re-editing the material and trying to decide how to use Terekhova further. He was also waiting to hear from a speech therapist, with whom he had arranged to film a live session (the healing of the stutterer). The first workbook ends with an extended version of the telephone conversation between the author and his mother, and

5. Margarita Terekhova as Maria, filming the external scenes of the printing-works episode in Moscow. (Photograph: Vladimir Murashko)

with Tarkovsky noting people's reaction to the material so far and wondering to himself: 'can it really be that a masterpiece is ripening? I don't feel it. I've already made this film.'

Tarkovsky's state of mind in early 1974 is evident from his diary, to which he gave the name *Martyrology*, adding under the title: 'pretentious and false as a title, but let it stay as a reminder of my insignificance – obscene and futile.' He began his second workbook on 2 January 1974, writing a monologue for the prologue of the film, and also developing the earring scene, looking for a motivation for Terekhova's hurried departure from the doctor's house. Filming continued throughout this period, with some additional scenes for the earring episode. On 12 February, Tarkovsky wrote in his workbook: 'Today there was a scandal. Rita cannot cut the chicken's head off. She also didn't like her scene with the Spaniards. She says she "understood nothing". We haven't shot a thing. I feel quite desperate, especially because I can see that something is not right in these scenes.' Tarkovsky spent the next few days working on the script, noting that he and Misharin had totally changed Terekhova's role. This involved added dialogue between Terekhova and the author, as well as a decision to have her speak some of the disputed monologue Misharin had written about the author's guilt in the hippodrome scene. Throughout this period Tarkovsky continued to re-edit the film's sequences, writing down the different versions he wanted to try. He was becoming concerned with the length of the film, fearing that more scandals would erupt when the bureaucrats found out that it was longer than planned. In early March, shooting was coming to an end; all that was left were a few scenes, including the killing of the chicken, the levitating woman and the session with the speech therapist. In his diary, Tarkovsky noted with annoyance that he would have to resort to choosing music because Eduard Artemiev, his composer, announced that he was too empty and depleted to compose any. Despite this, Tarkovsky seemed happy with the outcome of the film. He had also found out that someone from the Cannes Film Festival wanted to screen *Mirror* there that year, so he felt under added pressure to complete it in time.

By mid-March, everything had changed. When he watched the film, Tarkovsky disliked what he saw, calling it 'shit' in his workbook.

To his diary he admitted that things were going badly, that the material refused to come together and that Sizov, who had watched the film, understood nothing.

From this time on, Tarkovsky began his long and painful process of editing the film which, together with the changes demanded of him by the studio and Goskino, lasted until the end of that year. Tarkovsky worked at a dizzying pace; almost every day he wrote out a plan for a new edit, executed it, viewed it and immediately rejected it. Before the age of digital editing, this was quite a formidable and time-consuming task – sections of film had to be spliced and pasted together by hand. Sometimes Tarkovsky would be editing within the individual sequences, not just between them. In his first few edits, Tarkovsky divided the sequence of the Spaniards and the first dream. Some scenes with the Spaniards were moved to the beginning of the film, just before the printing-works episode, which was followed by some of the first dream. The dacha sequence was moved towards the end, just before the shooting-range episode. Only the earring sequence appeared stable; it remained near the end throughout every new version. By the fifth version, on 23 March 1974, Tarkovsky had realised that the scene with the stutterer would be effective as an epigraph (though later he moved it to the middle). This fifth edit was an important one as Tarkovsky was attempting to clarify some of the problematic points: the difference between the mother and Natalia, and the confusing episode with the Spaniards. He moved some of the dacha sequences to the beginning of the film and introduced Terekhova, as Natalia, early on, hoping that this would clarify the two different roles. He also attempted to simplify the episode with the Spaniards, writing in his workbook: 'Without psychological analysis, or emphasis on Luisa's memories. A very short description of the corrida, the dance, the slap, Luisa's exit, saying that Ernesto understood nothing in Spain, then the footage of Spanish children.'

In the next few versions, Tarkovsky moved both the printing works and the Spanish sequence towards the end of the film, after the shooting-range episode and the war footage. Then, after another long conversation with his editor, Tarkovsky wrote in his workbook: 'the thing is, we forgot about the author, about nostalgia, about the fact that the author remembers his mother after the dacha. And the poems? This, too, is nostalgia!' Yet Tarkovsky was afraid that the

film would not come together because it lacked a culminating episode
that would reflect the mother's difficult life. And although he himself
had always believed that to be the earring episode, he now began to
have doubts. Another thought that preoccupied him was whether the
entire war sequence (military instructor and footage) should remain
as one unit; he felt it crushed the mother and made her disappear.

On 8 April 1974 Tarkovsky showed Ermash and the artistic council
the thirteenth version of the film. He recorded the day in his workbook as 'a monumental scandal' and in his diary he wrote: 'There was
a scandal when we showed the material to Ermash, who understood
nothing.'[22] His wife Larisa, however, arranged a clandestine viewing
for the director of the Cannes Film Festival who was in Moscow at
the time, and who chose it for the festival. The studio bosses refused
to send it, ostensibly because it was not ready. By 12 April and the
sixteenth version, Tarkovsky was feeling happier, certain that 'only an
idiot will not understand what is going on'. This version is, in fact,
very close to the film as we know it today, with only minor additions.

The next recorded discussion at Mosfilm took place on 17 April
1974. Despite the unanimous praise it was given as a ground-breaking
cinematic work, opinions were split. Some people (notably Kremnev,
one of the film's staunchest supporters) believed that everything was
clear and beautifully linked together, and that attempting to explain
things further would kill the poetry and sense of mystery and beauty
the film exuded. Others felt that much was inexplicable, that there was
a sense of monotony and repetition in the shots, that the narrator and
poet read their lines without emotion, and that even Terekhova's acting
was dull and too even. Opinions varied also on the role of the poetry:
for some it was at odds with the image, interfering with their emotional
response to the events on the screen; others saw it as a beautifully
rendered commentary, interpretation even, of the unfolding images.
Tarkovsky agreed that poetry, in principle, has no place inside a film.
He noted, however, that the first poem we hear, while possibly destroy-
ing some of the sense of Maria's loneliness (one of the criticisms),
raises the scene out of the domestic realm, makes it more than mere
aestheticism. He admitted that the poem heard over the Sivash
sequence was perhaps less successful, but explained that since he
wanted some commentary, he preferred a poem to a text. The two
other main problem areas were: the episode with the Spaniards, which

most of those present found confusing and misplaced within the context of the film, and the final sequence. Tarkovsky, in this edit, used the sequence with himself in bed and the conversation with the doctor about the author's conscience. It seemed to the council that this sequence was attempting to interpret a film based on associations, memories and sensations, therefore striking a false note. They also objected – as previously – to Tarkovsky's presence. Naumov suggested that at least he show only his hand. Tarkovsky asked to be allowed to do a new mix, assuring them that much would become clearer then.

A month later, on 17 May, the artistic council met again, to watch a new edit with a new soundtrack. The main question was whether the general viewer would understand this film. The answer was a firm no. The council called for more clarity, wanting Tarkovsky to indicate which sequences were dreams and which reality, and to differentiate the roles of the actors, in the cases where he used the same actor for two different roles. He was also to devise a way of explaining to the viewers from the very beginning that this was to be a plotless film. Criticism continued over Tarkovsky's appearance at the end of the film, with Khutsiev protesting 'the "I" is the artist, not a first name and a surname',[23] because this would narrow the scope of the film. A letter dated 24 May, setting out eight recommendations, followed the meeting:

1. Clearly indicate the three layers of the film – present reality, reminiscences and dreams – and clarify the actors' roles in the cases where one actor plays two different people.
2. Either reshoot, or change through text and editing the episode with the shell-shocked instructor.
3. The war is not shown as promised, i.e. as a liberating mission. Highlight the patriotism of Soviet people. Use more war footage, and cut the nude images of soldiers from the Sivash sequence.
4. The mother's life is not adequately paralleled with the life of the nation. Reinstate the footage of the stratosphere balloon, include more footage of the Spanish Civil War and of Spanish children coming over to the Soviet Union and insert the May Day parade of 1939 on Red Square.
5. Clarify the fictional sequence with the Spaniards, which is out of context.

6. Conclude the earring episode with the heroine leaving the doctor's house, in order to show her disapproval of such material comfort during wartime.
7. Cut the shot of the levitating woman, which is baffling and unclear.
8. The author's appearance at the end of the film makes its contents too personal and raises aesthetic as well as ethical objections.

Tarkovsky responded by saying he would introduce inscriptions to specify the structure and the personages of the film, change the narrator's text in order to clarify – and partly change – the meaning of the film, and shorten several episodes.

According to Tarkovsky's workbook, one of the most dramatic meetings with the artistic council appears to have taken place around this time. Tarkovsky reports that Naumov started to scream at him: 'Genius, genius! They tell you you're a genius and you believe them! They tell you the film is a masterpiece and you believe them!' and ended by saying, 'Cursed be the day that Tarkovsky started making this film!' None of the above, of course, was transcribed for the Mosfilm archive.

Tarkovsky made two of the requested changes: cutting his face from the illness sequence and reinstating the stratosphere balloons, which had been dropped along the way. He also noted that he wanted to diversify the war footage by adding more, in chronological order (Hiroshima, Korea, Vietnam, Israel, China and Damansky island), in order to track the growing threat of war. And in his workbook he adds angrily: 'they want the life of the nation? They'll get it!' He spent most of June working on the soundtrack, adding more of the poetry to the film, re-editing the final sequence, the sequence at the shooting range and some of the archival footage. Though the film was initially supposed to be completed by 28 May, Sizov kept prolonging the editing period. Tarkovsky at this point felt that the film was ready; his main problem now had become the length of the film – should he opt for a longer or a shorter version?

On 24 June 1974 the artistic council met again to view the film, in Sizov's presence. Sizov asked Tarkovsky to cut two shots: the levitating woman, and his hand throwing up the bird, both of which he found baffling and meaningless. He also urged him to use more of the narrator's text, which he liked, but which disappeared for a large part of the film. They talked extensively about the documentary footage (which now included Hitler's corpse, Mao's China, Vietnam and Hiroshima) and about the sequence in the shooting range ending with the image of Asafiev and the little bird. Sizov thought that it should not form one whole unit, but should be broken up with footage in between so as to change the accent. He also wanted Tarkovsky to shorten the film, saying it was too long at 115 minutes, and that this would affect its distribution. Tarkovsky asked to show the film to Ermash, but Sizov suggested he first make some changes and then show it with the studio supporting him.

On 2 July 1974 Tarkovsky and members of the artistic council watched the film, which was now 130 minutes. Tarkovsky decided it looked terrible and returned to the editing table, determined to shorten it. In the next meeting, on 12 July, the film had shrunk to 112 minutes,

6. Tarkovsky and Terekhova during the filming of the controversial 'levitating woman' scene. (Photograph: Vladimir Murashko)

but people still felt it was drawn out. Sizov accused Tarkovsky of not having made any of the proposed changes. Of the shot of the levitating woman, which had not been cut, he said: 'We cannot have such biblical tendencies in a Soviet film.' He thought the Sivash footage showed political disloyalty, and that the film was a far cry from the original proposal. He was very critical of the sequence at the shooting gallery, feeling it denigrated the military instructor (Tarkovsky had included the following bit of dialogue by Asafiev: 'If you knew how to shoot you would not have ended up with a hole in your head'). After months of praise and support, suddenly the entire premise and language of the film was being questioned. Boris Pavlenok, the vice-president of Goskino and Dal Orlov, a film-critic, sided with Sizov, also drawing attention to biblical tendencies in the conversation between Natalia and the author about the burning bush. Khutsiev and Kremnev tried to defend Tarkovsky, who was understandably shocked and incredulous at the accusations. Sizov told Tarkovsky plainly that if he did not make the changes required of him – 'the absolute ideological minimum' – the film would not be accepted by the studio, and he would have to show it to Ermash alone.

Ermash took part in the discussion on 25 July. Tarkovsky's 'comrades' at Mosfilm tried to present a united front, attempting to strike a balance between identifying the film's problem areas and praising Tarkovsky's work and commitment. Ermash remained unimpressed and unpersuaded. 'Unfortunately,' he said, 'Andrei Arsenevich did not fulfil the promises he gave when he started making this film. This is a totally different film.' He added that he could not accept the film in its present form – pronouncing it 'sheer rebus' – and that it should be re-edited for the purposes of clarity. He called attention to the choice of Bach, saying that the use of his religious music gave the film a mystical character, which was very un-Soviet. Tarkovsky protested that this was the very greatest music ever composed. Ermash listed several points that needed urgent attention, which were reiterated in a letter sent the following day:

1. Cut the opening sequence with the speech therapist and stutterer.
2. Re-edit the episode at the shooting range, removing the instructor's stuttering and the pupils' mocking attitude towards him.
3. Remove the sad tone of the 'Spanish' episode, and emphasise the

joy of the Spanish children over coming to the Soviet Union. Remove the footage of the stratosphere balloon.

4. Cut some of the Pushkin letter, as well as the mystical ending of the sequence.

5. Remove the hints and innuendoes about the nature of the publication from the printing-works episode, shorten the long walks through the spaces.

6. Re-examine the war footage, taking chronology into account. Do not edit the Second World War with Vietnam. The parade in Peking does not fit in with the rest of the material. The entire footage should be separated into two parts, the first concentrating entirely on the Second World War.

7. Some of the dialogue involving Natalia has a biblical tone. It should be re-mixed and motivated by plot.

8. The metaphorical scene of the levitating woman is unpersuasive and should be removed.

9. The narrator's text is too pessimistic, we have a sense that he lived his life in vain, unable to express himself in his art. Introduce text to the opposite effect.

10. Relieve the entire film of mysticism.[24]

Tarkovsky would not fulfil these requests, but he had to make some changes. So he removed the 'sadness' from the 'Spanish' episode, not by showing happy meetings between Spaniards and Soviets, but by inserting footage of the triumphant return of Chkalov from his flight over the North Pole. He also added footage of Soviet troops entering Prague, to quench the calls for more optimism and heroism. He edited all the footage in chronological order, as had been requested of him. He shortened, but did not remove, the long-disputed sequence of the levitating woman, and said he would write some more text for the narrator at the end of the film, clarifying his thoughts for the future; they were, 'Never mind. Everything will be all right.'

Tarkovsky continued to fight over the film. In early August 1974 he drew up a campaign plan in his diary, involving writing letters to Ermash and Sizov about his work situation and organising a screening for influential figures (among them Shostakovich) who might sign a petition in support of the film. If all this failed and Ermash rejected the film, he contemplated writing to Brezhnev. His final thought was to ask permission to go abroad for two years, to make a film there. In the Soviet Union at this time, a period of oppression and rejection reigned throughout the cinema world. Sergei Paradzhanov had just been jailed for five years, a series of films were being shelved, productions closed down, and Tarkovsky wrote in his diary that Romanov had been an angel compared to Ermash. He feared that *Mirror* too would be shelved. At the end of August Sizov finally decided to have a print of the film made, yet calls for changes – and the threat of a possible 'shelving' – continued throughout September. Finally, on 22 October 1974, the film was accepted; Tarkovsky recorded this in his workbook and concluded: 'and so the saga ends.'

On 13 November 1974, the artistic council met again, to cast a vote on whether the film would be given first or second category (see 'The Reception of the Film'). *Mirror* fell one vote short of first category. But Tarkovsky's next diary entry at the end of 1974 was about the success of *Mirror* which 'has demonstrated to me yet again how well founded was my conjecture about the importance of personally experienced emotion in telling a story from the screen. Perhaps cinema is the most personal art, the most intimate. In cinema only the author's intimate truth will be convincing enough for the audience to accept',[25] and about reports from some leading critics of the time that the film was a work of genius.

Notes

1. Spoken by the head of Goskino, Filipp Ermash, after he watched *Mirror* for the first time. Quoted in A. Misharin, 'Na krovi, kul'ture i istorii', in *O Tarkovskom* (Moscow, 1989), p. 63.

2. *Kogda fil'm okonchen. Govoriat rezhissery 'Mosfil'ma* (Moscow, 1964), pp. 136–71. A revised version was included as the chapter 'The Beginning', in A. Tarkovsky, *Sculpting in Time. Reflections on the Cinema* (London, 1986), pp. 15–35.

3. A. Konchalovskii, *Nizkie istiny* (Moscow, 1998), pp. 126–7.

4. Tarkovsky, *Sculpting in Time. Reflections on the Cinema* (London, 1986), p. 128.

5. A. Tarkovskii, *Uroki rezhissury* (Moscow, 1993), p. 28.

6. A. Tarkovskii, 'Belyi den'', *Iskusstvo kino*, 6, 1970, pp. 110–11.

7. See A. Tarkovsky, *Collected Screenplays* (London, 1999), pp. 257–61.

8. A literary script reads like a story, as opposed to the shooting script,

which usually indicates metres of film, type of shot and lens, a sound-track and drawings.

9. Misharin, 'Na krovi, kul'ture i istorii ...', pp. 55–66.

10. A hybrid script was published in Russian and translated into English, included in *Collected Screenplays*, pp. 251–321. This contains elements of the early script as well as some of the episodes in the film.

11. This scene echoes one in *Nostalgia* where Gorchakov looks into a mirrored wardrobe to find Domenico staring back at him. It also re-sembles a scene from Tarkovsky's unfilmed script on the life of E. T. A. Hoffmann, *Hoffmanniana*, where Hoffmann, in his delirium, sees his double, Cavalier Gluck. See Tarkovsky, *Collected Screenplays*, pp. 329–69.

12. Mosfilm, 2264.

13. Tarkovsky, *Time within Time*, p. 13.

14. See *Collected Screenplays*, pp. 187–247.

15. The battle of Kulikovo took place in 1380 between Prince Dmitri Don-skoi and the Mongols, and dealt a decisive blow to their long rule over Russia. This episode originally belonged to the script of *Andrei Rublev*, but was deemed too costly and never filmed.

16. From the unpublished version of the Russian diary, held at the Institut Tarkovski in Paris.

17. Tarkovsky, *Time within Time*, p. 62.

18. Ibid., p. 65.

19. From the unpublished version of the Russian diary.

20. From Tarkovsky's first workbook on *Mirror*, held at the Institut Tar-kovski in Paris.

21. This and quotes that follow are from Mosfilm 519/10/34.

22. From the unpublished version of the Russian diary.

23. This and quotes that follow are from Mosfilm 520/10/34.

24. This document has been published in V. Fomin, 'Vse nerazreshennoe-zapreshcheno', *Iskusstvo kino*, 5, 1989, p. 103. It is dated 3 July 1974 yet according to the Mosfilm archive, these points were mentioned by Er-mash on 25 July 1974.

25. Tarkovsky, *Time within Time*, p. 101.

3. *Mirror*: An Analysis

7. The Gorchakovs' dacha near the village of Ignatievo, 1935. Maria Tarkovskaia is pictured, with Andrei, Marina and a friend in the foreground. (Photograph: Lev Gornung)

Preparations for Filming *Mirror*

'At the dacha the buckwheat blossomed', wrote Tarkovsky in his workbook on 9 July 1973. The contents of this rather cryptic sentence carried great meaning for him. The dacha in question is the one where the young mother lives with her children and where the childhood dreams take place. The original dacha, near the village of Ignatievo, no longer existed. But Tarkovsky set about rebuilding it, relying not only on his child's memory of it, but also on the tangible evidence of its existence – family photographs. This is where Lev Gornung, a largely unknown protagonist in the creative process of *Mirror*, makes his entrance. He and Tarkovsky's father met in Moscow in 1928, just after the latter's marriage to Maria Vishniakova. The three remained friends until the end of their lives, and Gornung became their children's godfather. The descendant of a Swedish family of seafarers who had come to Russia during the reign of Peter the Great, he also wrote poetry, and was a gifted photographer. It was he who photographed the Tarkovsky family constantly in those early years. It was also he who suggested that the Tarkovskys spend the summer of 1935 near the village of Ignatievo, at the dacha of Pavel Gorchakov. This house is the one Tarkovsky re-created for the film, the recurring house of his dreams (see also '*Mirror*'s Chronotopes', p. 10).

Tarkovsky grew up with these photographs, with a tangible sense of the child he once was and the world he once inhabited; a tactile, immediate visual reality, which his artistic sensibility would penetrate and relive, in order to capture and reinterpret its essence. The images from these photographs permeate much of *Mirror*. Tarkovsky not only re-created the structures, but also the clothes, the objects, the poses, the quality of light, and the invisible tensions and connections that exist between the people pictured: the Tarkovsky family. He studied these photographs very closely when preparing and shooting the film; they covered the walls of his workroom at Mosfilm, and his study at home. He distributed them to his assistants, when they were looking for actors, props and costumes. Lev Gornung had sold two hundred of his negatives to Mosfilm, for a pittance, and with the promise of a full set of prints, which he never received. By that time he had lost his eyesight and could not witness the effect of his work

8. Lev Gornung at the Gorchakovs' dacha, summer 1935. Behind him, under construction, is the shed that burnt down some time later, an event Tarkovsky re-creates in *Mirror*. (Photograph: Maria Tarkovskaia)

in *Mirror*. He was the Tarkovsky family 'chronicler' and Andrei's benign godfather, a humble presence, whose remarkable contribution has remained largely unacknowledged.

The process of re-creating the past for Tarkovsky began with re-building the idealised house of his childhood. Guided by the photographs, he built an exact replica of the Gorchakovs' house, on the original foundations, taking care to use old wooden logs, in order to create the texture and indelible presence of time. He went even further, asking members of the local kolkhoz to sow part of the field in front of the house with buckwheat, whose white flowers were an inextricable part of his childhood. They protested that for many years only clover and oats had grown there, and that the soil was quite wrong for buckwheat. But when it *did* blossom, Tarkovsky took it as a sign: 'It was an illustration of the emotional quality of our memory, of its ability to penetrate the veils concealed by time, and this is exactly what we wanted to express through the film. I don't know what would have happened to the film if the buckwheat had not blossomed. This was immensely important to me.'[1] When everything was ready, Tarkovsky took his mother to see the house and was reassured by her reaction.

The choice of location has always been of utmost importance to Tarkovsky; he believed that if he was moved by a certain location, if it awakened in him a series of memories and associations, then it could not fail to move the audience. With *Mirror*, the process went even deeper, as his task was to re-create something that had once been an inextricable part of his reality. And Tarkovsky, who had always been very demanding of his collaborators, requested their absolute commitment to his new project. In *Sculpting in Time*[2] he gives an account of the atmosphere on set, of how the crew spent all their time together, speaking about intimate things, and immersing themselves in the atmosphere of the film and its characters. Tarkovsky and Rerberg worked hard over each shot, in order to express the optimum truth in the particular moment of life they were committing to film; they looked at the way the landscape changed with the light, how the different times of day and variations in the weather influenced the surrounding reality. The river's current, its colour, depth and waterweeds had to be considered if the actors would be walking past it in a take – everything that might 'live' in a shot was examined. Tarkovsky made sure that there was sand and dust residue in the white enamel basin that was to gather the rain, and carefully placed two chicken feathers by it. He always set up the shot composition himself, carefully attending to the tiniest detail. He relished this aspect of production and was for ever gathering objects that he liked, thinking that he might use them in some future mise-en-scène.

While still working on the shooting script, Tarkovsky, Misharin and Rerberg spent two entire days with the production designer, Nikolai Dvigubsky, unable to continue, because they could not decide what plant should grow in the garden between the house and the burning shed. Dvigubsky finally came up with the potato plant, whose yellow-lilac flowers would give the shots the density they required. Tarkovsky went as far as to have three versions of the same dress made for the mother, each with a different colour tone, in order to communicate the changing light of day, the place of action and the heroine's mood more precisely in each scene. He made sure that the red-head, depicted in war-time, wore an ill-fitting coat, passed down from someone else. The bonnet Alexei's sister wears in the scene of the meeting with their father was identical to the one Tarkovsky's sister, Marina, wore in the war years, made by their grandmother from old plush. Tarkovsky consulted war experts before creating the military instructor's head wound, to make it as authentic as possible, down to the plastic cap he wears under his army one in order to protect it. Each frame, each reconstructed memory and emotion had to sound a truthful note; no means was spared to achieve this. Margarita Terekhova was never given the script, only her daily scenes, because he did not want her to know what really happened to the character of the mother – namely, that the husband she is waiting for at the beginning of the film will never return. He wanted her to live through the moment as his mother once had, unaware of her fate.

Another unusual aspect of filming *Mirror* was that Tarkovsky utterly cast aside the shooting script once he was on set. He and Misharin would write new scenes and snippets of dialogue every day; these would go into the next day's shooting schedule. Misharin remembers the film's story editor constantly running after him, begging for a piece of paper, anything that might hint at what they were going to shoot next; Tarkovsky, meanwhile, would run to the set with countless

9. Maria Tarkovskaia in Zavrazhe, Tarkovsky's birthplace, 1932.
(Photograph: Lev Gornung)

10. Terekhova as Maria, watching the shed burn while sitting at the well, which Tarkovsky 'borrowed' from the Zavrazhe photograph. (Photograph: Vladimir Murashko)

scraps of paper and shoot according to them. After all, he had always maintained that film scripts were simply an occasion for reflection, that they should 'die' in the film. *Mirror* would grow organically out of its milieu, location, conditions of filming, and the actors' and director's moods; as Tarkovsky had intended it.

Tarkovsky's Cinematic Language: Formal Aspects of *Mirror*

In 1985, the year before he died, Tarkovsky said in an interview that *Mirror* was the film closest to his concept of cinema. Indeed, it was the gathering place of all his aesthetic and ethical concerns in his chosen medium; his beliefs about the film frame, about rhythm, editing and mise-en-scène, but also about artistic responsibility and human conscience all find a voice in this film. The prologue, in which the stutterer is finally able to pronounce 'I can speak' unhindered, suggests more than an emotional emancipation – it announces the artist's mastering of his craft, and the unique freedom he enjoys in having done so. There is a tremendous freedom at the heart of *Mirror*: an ease of associations, a constant ebb and flow in the images, an abundance of references, textures, spaces, movements, and passages of suspended motion. More than anything, it resembles a musical composition; it is polyphonic in its use of its disparate parts, but the sense of wholeness and harmony it creates makes it akin to a symphony. Tarkovsky always maintained that he used the laws of music as the film's organising principle. He considered film to have much in common with a musical ordering of material, where emphasis was placed not on the *logic*, but on the *form*, of the flow of events. And form for him was ultimately linked to time – the duration and the passage of time in each shot. But he did not approach time as an abstract, philosophical concept; rather, it was an inner psychological reality and he believed that one of the aims of the film director was to create his unique sense of time in a film, which was independent of real time.

If time was one side of the coin, memory was the other. For Tarkovsky the two were inextricable; time produced memory, which, in its turn, allowed one to move freely in time. And cinema was called to raise, in Proust's words, 'a vast edifice of memories'. To do that it had to work with time. Tarkovsky's definition of cinema as 'a sculpture made of time' informs every aspect of his film-making: camera, decor, mise-en-scène, texture, rhythm and editing. Each shot, each sequence, imprints time.[3] We have already seen how thorough and meticulous he was in establishing each shot. He knew that by combining different elements, textures and objects in a single frame he could alter the face and flow of time, and create distinct time-pressures within each shot. This was his means of arriving at *rhythm*, which he saw as the main formative element of a film. In his writings, he demoted the importance of editing in favour of rhythm, asserting that all the qualities of a film existed in the individual shots, and editing was merely the ideal version of their assembly, almost an afterthought – though one that all but destroyed *Mirror*.

Tarkovsky was full of paradoxes and contradictions, which are beautifully assimilated in *Mirror*. While advocating an attendance to one's inner sense of time, and the creation of a distinctly unique personal reality, he also said that the cinematic image is, 'essentially, the observation of a fact flowing in time'[4] and stated his partiality towards documentary and newsreel, which he saw as a way of reconstructing, re-creating life. In *Mirror*, he was able to marry fact with fiction, personal with real time, by including documentary footage in its structure. This, in turn, affected the film's rhythm and editing, as it called for a synthesis of very different time-pressures and filming techniques. And although Tarkovsky sided with the artists who could discern what he called 'the poetic design of being', and convey 'the deep complexity and truth of the impalpable connections and hidden phenomena of life', he also posited that 'unless there exists an organic link between the subjective impressions of the author and his objective representation of reality, he will fail to achieve even superficial credibility, let alone authenticity and inner truth'.[5] Many people will rightly argue that Tarkovsky's representation of reality is anything but objective, yet his brand of objectivity lies in his rendering of the material world – landscape, objects, textures, qualities of light and colour. He wanted the work to be an exact factual account and a true communication of feelings. The strength of his films, but especially of *Mirror*, is that they give form, density and a particular 'voice' to an aspect of life that language is not capable of. And the contradictions – personal and real time, fact and fiction, reconstruction and authenticity – are what make this film his most polyphonic work.

The most distinct aspect of Tarkovsky's cinematic vocabulary is his representation of dream, vision and memory on screen; these different layers of consciousness make up most of *Mirror*, and the boundaries between them in this film are extremely tenuous. The director was categorically against the usual fades, hazy screens or musical passages that, all too often in films, signal the beginning of a dream or memory. The logic of the dream for him consisted of 'unusual and unexpected combinations of, and conflicts between, entirely real elements'.[6] He used several devices to achieve this, some of which are well illustrated by the first childhood dream in *Mirror*. This, like the following two, is filmed in monochrome and takes place at night in the dacha. Young Alexei, sleeping in a large iron bed, suddenly wakes up. Then we see a shot of the edge of the forest, out of which comes a powerful gust of wind. Here Tarkovsky combines elements of the natural world in an unusual way – a gust of wind would never escape from a forest like that. It is as though a disembodied being has pushed its way out of the forest's darkness; it suggests a mysterious, living presence, and also appears to be a message for Alexei who calls out 'Papa!' From then on, this strange wind becomes associated with the much-coveted figure of the father. In the sequence that follows – the mother's washing of her hair – the director uses another method: the spatial and temporal dislocation of a character, so characteristic of the architecture of dreams. In a lateral tracking shot the camera follows Maria as she walks towards the left side of the room, tracks past her and her mirrored reflection, leaving them both to the right side of the frame, then picks her up again on the left side of the frame, giving the impression that she exists simultaneously in two different areas of the room. Maria then disappears from the frame to be replaced by an old woman (played by Tarkovsky's mother), her future self, wearing the same shawl as her. Tarkovsky uses this device often, to suggest that past, present and future exist simultaneously, that time and space are not subject to the laws of logic. In the same sequence, he introduces a series of natural and man-made elements, each of which has its own texture and density. Rain falls inside the room, the walls have been eroded by water and the ceiling is collapsing. As the entire sequence is filmed in slow motion, we are able to experience the *weight* of the ceiling plaster as it splashes on to a water-filled floor, the *fragility* of the small flame burning on the stove in a corner, the *lightness* of the rain, as it falls on to Maria's shoulders. Maria herself is transformed into a willow-like shape[7] as she stands in the middle of the room in her white nightdress, her wet hair thrown forward and her arms suspended in mid-air, swaying imperceptibly. The unreality and strangeness of the sequence comes from the marriage of real elements and shapes. Nothing is artificial; we know the texture, shape, weight and sound of everything that we see on the screen, but the result is surprising, magical and inexplicable.

Another striking feature of Tarkovsky's cinematic language is the kinaesthetic quality of his films. He loved long tracking shots, which he used extensively. At times his camera tracks and zooms simultaneously, or it circles an object, attempting to render it from all possible angles. It is hardly ever still; sometimes it deceives us into thinking that it is still, when in fact it is tracking imperceptibly. This has the effect of drawing the viewer inside the frame, affording him a visceral experience. The mesmerising camera movements, together with the unusual events taking place within the frame, confound all attempts to interpret the image. The emphasis is on directly experiencing it and allowing it to affect a deeper layer of our consciousness. The camera is used as a probe; by fixing its gaze so relentlessly on the surrounding reality, it seeks to uncover its hidden meaning. Tarkovsky's long takes, slow and sustained tracking shots and close-ups affect the ways we perceive the image. His camera, often trained on an object for an unusually lengthy screen-time, allows a transformation to take place. It forces us to contemplate it, it exposes the matter it is made of and allows us to see what lies beyond the surface. Another device he uses (particularly in the dreams) is slow motion, but at times it is almost unnoticeable. In the printing-works sequence, for example, he uses it several times when filming Maria and Liza, but it affects our senses before it does our cognition; we have a sensation of a certain dislocation, of something odd, but we cannot quite pinpoint it.

Colour is another formal element of *Mirror*, though the colour coding does not observe any strict rules, and was mostly a result of limited colour stock. Most of the dreams and visions are in monochrome; not all the memories are, and nor is it always easy to distinguish between the three. The levitating woman could be either a dream or a vision; the red-head by the burning stove and her hand shielding the burning branch could be any of the three. The footage is monochrome and black-and-white. Not all the reconstructed, fictional episodes are in colour; the sequence at the printing works blends monochrome with black-and-white; the final scene between Natalia and Alexei in his flat is monochrome. Very often, the colour-sequences are all but drained of colour. This occurs in the scenes inside the narrator's flat and in the episode at the shooting range, whose predominant colour is the white of snow. The scenes in and around the dacha have a warm and gentle quality to them. Nothing is ever bright; even the fire is somehow toned down. Tarkovsky frames it, contains it within the forest, juxtaposes it with rain, does not allow it to run wild. And this brings us to what is perhaps the director's most important pronouncement on the creation of form, and the key to understanding the aesthetic and psychological language of *Mirror*: 'The artist has a duty to be calm. He has no right to show his emotion, his involvement, to go pouring it all out at the audience. Any excitement over a subject must be sublimated into an Olympian calm of form. That is the only way in which an artist can tell of the things that excite him.'[8] This Olympian calm of form is what prompted those of Tarkovsky's colleagues who were expecting intense scenes between the protagonists to call the film dull; it is what turns the burning shed from a destructive accident into an epiphany, and why the grenade the military instructor throws himself on is a dummy. It makes the quarrel between the two women in the printing works unfold through Dostoevsky, and compels the Spaniard to hit his daughter when he discovers that she can dance flamenco. It does not allow us to track motivation or outcome because there is no logical development; there is only the image, framed, and the torturous emotion, arrested in time. Tarkovsky admired Chekhov for removing the first page of his stories, in order to eradicate the *why*. He himself removes pages throughout the story, leaving us with fragments, whose meaning and motivation is not easily decipherable. We are left instead with a feeling for a particular mood, atmosphere or emotion – and a world of juxtapositions and correspondences, to which we must bring to bear our own sensibility.

A Word About Editing *Mirror*

The editing phase of *Mirror* was, as we have seen, a seven-month battle, which threatened Tarkovsky daily with utter defeat. He felt that the material refused to be edited together, that it made no sense at all, and this led him to believe that there was something inherently wrong with what he had filmed. His approach to editing, but particularly to editing *Mirror*, can, without exaggeration, be characterised as mystical. He believed that he could not impose his will or logic on the material, he had to let *it* speak to him and guide him. He must be able to divine its rhythm, by paying attention to the time-pressure of each shot, but he must also, like the musician, have an 'ear' for the false notes. Tarkovsky maintained that certain shots cannot be edited together because they feel 'false', and therefore do not sit well next to those that are organic. In his film lectures, he illustrated this by describing his failed attempts to edit a shot into the Spanish Civil War footage – that of a soldier kissing his weeping child goodbye as it boarded a Soviet ship. Trying to fathom why the shot would not mix with the others, Tarkovsky watched all the footage he had been given on the subject, and found three takes of that particular scene. Authenticity had been sacrificed to propaganda and the shot would not fit. Tarkovsky also disliked all manner of prettiness and suggestiveness in a scene; he reportedly shortened the episode of the father's return on furlough and the sale of the earrings because someone commented on how beautiful they were.

Tarkovsky's removal of motivation and development, as well as the gradual way in which the material came together – with the eleventh-hour decision to create the role of Natalia, Alexei's wife, and the painstaking search for documentary footage – all made editing *Mirror* such a daunting task. Tarkovsky never had a version of the completed film either in his head, or on paper; he only ever had a sense of what he wanted to express. It is interesting to note that his long-time editor, Liudmila Feiginova, gave a very different, less dramatic, account of the editing of the film. She said that the essential structure of the film did not change significantly through the twenty-one edits. The beginning and the end had always been in place, except for the sequence with the stutterer, which Tarkovsky initially wanted to show from the television screen, somewhere in the middle of the film. Feiginova argued that it was too long to take place inside a small screen, saying she could not cut it effectively ('the film-stock protests' were her words) and should be introduced, in its entirety, either at the beginning or at the end. Another suggestion she made was also vital for the film, and revealing of her working relationship with Tarkovsky. She felt that the Sivash footage was too long if accompanied only by music, so she thought of laying one of Arseni Tarkovsky's poems over it;[9] this would concentrate the viewers' attention and encourage their emotions away from possible thoughts on the origin of the images. When she mentioned her idea to Tarkovsky, he mocked her, but she insisted they try it. Then she deliberately misaligned the poem to the image, so that Tarkovsky would involve himself in the process, try it out for himself and, she hoped, come round to her idea. This is what happened, and the poem finally found its ideal place within the sequence.

Tarkovsky's sense of urgency over the editing had to do not only with his personal connection to the material, but also with the critical stance of his 'comrades' at the studio. As the requests for cuts and calls for clarification were never-ending, the battle took place on two fronts: with the material and with the authorities. What might the film have looked like, one wonders, if criticism had not been so harsh and so loud? If Tarkovsky had been left alone to decide at which point *he* was satisfied with it? The extended use of documentary footage came out of calls for more historical context; in the end, it enriched the film, but that is because Tarkovsky searched hard for unusual and unknown sequences, and was rewarded with the discovery of the Sivash footage. The fictional sequences were also transformed by the constant attacks. An example of one is Maria's 'levitating scene'. This sequence, which was silent initially, provoked bewilderment and accusations of mysticism. Tarkovsky would either have to explain it in some way, or cut it out. The explanation was the added dialogue between Maria and the father, where she tells him that she has 'flown up' like that because she loves him. A very important part of the editing process was the aural realm – music, dialogue, voice-over, sounds – for it too influenced the emphasis and rhythm of the visual language of the film.

Despite the commonly held opinion that *Mirror* is a labyrinthine film, if we examine the way it is put together, we will be surprised at the logic behind its final form. What on first viewing appear to be randomly joined episodes, prove to have both motivation and sequentiality. The prologue proclaims the film's confessional tone and the discovery of a method – the *means* by which the artist will speak. It is set up, but not acted out; it is merely fixed on the film stock as a document – indeed, as a fact flowing in time. It is a fact, which is sublimated into a metaphor by its very significance in the context of what follows. What follows is a freely constructed essay on memory and history. The film proper begins with a slow forward tracking shot, *into* the story/memory, while the lens zooms out momentarily even as the camera is moving forward. This opposing movement creates an estranging effect; we are being slowly taken in, but also kept on the threshold. The voice-over sets the scene up as a memory, even as it is played out before us in real time. The telephone call that follows suggests the sequence might have been a dream/memory, as the narrator tells his mother he had just been dreaming of her and of himself as a boy. It also gives motivation for the printing-works sequence, which is brought on by the mother mentioning her colleague, Liza's, death. The scenes between the narrator and Natalia also move the narrative forward, commenting, directly or indirectly, on the sequences they precede. In the narrator's flat, his Spanish guests also remember a childhood broken by war and farewells. The attendant footage tells us something about their own tragedy: their civil war, loss of home and migration to the Soviet Union. This otherwise 'superfluous' sequence in fact sets up a parallel with the author's own experience. His guests' lives have been as devastated as his own has by war and family separation. The strange visitation of the two women at the flat introduces a page from the Russian past, while Ignat's telephone conversation with his father propels us into one of the darkest moments of world history: the Second World War. The sequence at the shooting range that follows begins innocently enough through Alexei telling his son of the red-head he was in love with as a young boy (we realise that hers is the hand that appears shielding a burning branch several times throughout the film). Yet, as it progresses, it reveals the terrible damage of war on the individual soul. The footage within it, though, shows not only conflict and loss, but also heroism and victory. The emotions and deprivations of war-time are developed further in the next two sequences: the mother and children's quietly overwhelming meeting with the father, who is visiting them while on furlough, and the attempted sale of the earrings to the rich doctor's wife. This is another mute expression of hardship, humility and pride. The film ends by asserting harmony and love, a time before and after tragedy. All the main characters are present, in their past and in their future, and the camera, in a beautiful reverse movement to that of the opening sequence, tracks away from them, into the forest. Even as it is doing so, it zooms in for a brief moment, unwilling to let go of that distant happiness. The film is delicately framed between these two 'mirrored' tracking shots, and its constant shifts are propelled by an invisible thread, which is far more consequential than might initially be perceived.

The Aural Realm

Three distinct aural layers shape *Mirror*: music, sound effects and voice-over, which includes the poems read by Arseni Tarkovsky. If we were to watch the film with our attention focused on the sound-track, we would be surprised at just how extensive the use of sound and electronic music is. The fact that this is not immediately obvious is evidence of the organic way it has been married to the image. This bears out Tarkovsky's belief that music should be so integrated with the image that, were we to remove it, the image would be qualitatively different. It especially pertains to the electronic sounds created for the film by Eduard Artemiev. Tarkovsky had first worked with him on *Solaris*, fascinated by the immense possibilities that electronic music seemed to hold. He believed that if 'purged of its chemical origins', this music could capture the 'primary notes of the world', and reproduce 'precise states of mind, the sounds of a person's interior world'.[10] In *Mirror*, this is beautifully demonstrated. The electronic music gives presence to invisible things (the wind escaping from out of the forest), it expresses ominousness and epiphany (the childhood dreams, the fire in the shed, the falling ceiling) and warns of unexpected occurrences (the boy getting an electric shock when picking up a coin, followed by the appearance of the two women). The sounds can be quite diverse: harsh and metallic (the electric shock brought on by the coin), a rumbling (the fire, the wind), the sound of bells and imperceptible voices (the falling ceiling) and even choral passages (the reading of Pushkin's letter). At times the music is almost symphonic (the children's reunion with the father), while at others it is pared down to variations on one chord (the percussive/choral accompaniment to the Sivash footage). In the final dream, the music is best described as aleatoric.

Artemiev – contradicting Tarkovsky – recalls that initially there was no talk of composing music especially for *Mirror*, but that circumstances later changed and he ended up writing music, which Tarkovsky kept turning down. One thing that was certain (also based on Feiginova's evidence) was Tarkovsky's intent to keep the Sivash sequence silent, but for the sound of the soldiers' feet in the muddy water. Like Feiginova, Artemiev also thought that the sequence needed something more, and he wrote music, which Tarkovsky finally used, but without foregrounding it as the composer had intended. Artemiev said that Tarkovsky never spoke precisely about how he wanted the music to sound; rather, he spoke of the emotional tone of the film, and gave him total freedom to create it. Tarkovsky referred to the early shots, the childhood dreams and the wind rushing through the trees, saying that he wanted a sound that would evoke a mood of childhood fears and nightmares. Artemiev tried out various electronic sounds, but Tarkovsky was dissatisfied. Tarkovsky himself came up with the idea of using a simple child's pipe, whose haunting sound permeates so much of *Mirror*. In fact, Artemiev created not a musical composition, but a realm of sound, which underlay the image and was suggestive of an invisible, but existing reality. Tarkovsky used this as a further way of animating nature and bestowing numinousness upon phenomena. He wanted the world to resonate with a chthonic, inner echo, to surprise us with a universe of sound different from the one we are accustomed to hearing, and identifying objects with. In *Mirror*, the sound is frequently extraneous to the image. We hear, but never see, train whistles, dogs barking, bells, birds and trams. They fill the frame, implying that the known world surrounds the events we witness, but at the same time dislocating the events themselves. Tarkovsky continues this dislocation in other ways too: the fire and the wind do not crackle and hum respectively – they rumble. Sound is also spatially dislocated: we see rain falling at the back of the frame, yet we hear it in the foreground; a character is speaking at the end of a corridor, yet their voice is near, it fills the frame. Particular sounds dominate certain sequences: the printing works is permeated by brisk footsteps, Maria's laboured breath and the rhythmic sound of the printing presses; at the shooting range we are constantly aware of the distinct sound of heavy boots stepping on dense snow. These sounds dominate the frame, they do not remain in the background; they are akin to a musical refrain, creating a specific texture and mood and revealing more than words. In the printing-works episode, Tarkovsky further 'estranges' the images by marrying the real sound of the women's footsteps to their bodies gliding down corridors in imperceptible slow-motion – we hear them walk, but watch them glide. In mapping out the aural terrain, Tarkovsky observes an inner logic and necessity, in order to guide us past phenomena, to the noumena – the domain he and his father advocate in this film, found 'on the other side of the mirror'.

Apart from the voice-over, and the use of poetry, which we will look at in a separate section, two more expressions of the aural world are present in *Mirror*: classical music and, to a lesser degree, silence. Although Tarkovsky believed that if we learned to listen to, and organise, the sounds of the world effectively, there would be no use for music in the cinema, at the same time he felt that, as a young art, the cinema needed support from the older, well-established arts. Classical music, and especially the music of Bach, is one of Tarkovsky's beloved cultural and cinematic 'quotations'. Of all his films, *Mirror* has the most extensive and varied use of classical music: Bach, Purcell and Pergolesi. His choice of works – Pergolesi's Stabat Mater, extracts from Bach's St John and St Matthew Passions, and from the organ works – led to accusations of religiosity and mysticism. For Tarkovsky, this was music he knew and loved; it constituted part not only of his personal world, but also of the cultural history of humanity, and of its highest expressions of faith. It is present in the film as an attempt to place the unfolding events in a larger canvas. Tarkovsky knew that classical music, especially of that stature, was too autonomous to dissolve inside a film and become an organic part of it. His use of it celebrates this autonomy, for he applies it not in order to illustrate, but to transform the visual world. The Pergolesi fragment over the flight of the stratosphere balloons gives them gravity and context. The Purcell and Bach that respectively accompany the red-head walking in the snow and Alexei studying his face in the mirror, map a personal revelation: first love in the former case, and a quiet stirring of the inner self in the latter. As for the recitative and choral passages from Bach's Passions, it is interesting to speculate whether Tarkovsky chose them purely on the strength of the music, or whether his choice was precipitated by the text sung at that particular point. His thoroughness would indicate that it was. The passage from the St Matthew Passion, played over the father's un-expected homecoming and the portrait of Ginevra de Benci, comes at the moment of Christ's death on the Cross: 'And behold, the veil of the temple was rent in twain, from the top to the bottom, and the earth did quake, and the rocks rent. And the graves were opened, and there arose many bodies of the saints which had slept.' This earth-shattering event in the history of Western religion is paralleled with one that seems to have had equal importance in the young Tarkovsky's memory – the father's safe return from the front. The film ends with the opening chorus from the St John Passion: 'Lord our master, whose glory fills the whole earth, show us by your Passion that you, the true eternal son of God, triumph even in the deepest humiliation.' The circular movement of this ecstatic piece of music affirms for Tarkovsky the cyclical nature of life, the presence of time past in time future, and the redeeming and transforming powers of art, which bestow grace and hope upon ailing humanity; it is an affirmation of faith and harmony. But Tarkovsky does not end the film there; after the music is over, and young Alexei has let out his affirming ululation, he returns us to silence. It is a pregnant silence, which we are called to fill in, not merely the fading out of the soundtrack. Is it the silence of nature, the silence enveloping the artist after his creative effort, or is it the ominous silence of an unknown threat? We are left to make that choice, while the camera, retreating into the forest, returns us to Dante's words.

Culture and History

Alexander Misharin remembers Tarkovsky saying to him: 'I can make something good based on three things only – blood, culture and history.'[11] For Tarkovsky, culture and history are part of the common roots of humanity, of its great triumphs and its terrible failures, all of which shape and inform successive generations. His cultural references, his beloved 'quotations' – works of painters, composers and poets – are a familiar part of his cinematic vocabulary and are present in most of his films. It was important for him to draw from such sources, not only in order to enrich his chosen medium, but also because, as an artist, he felt that his spiritual roots were not confined to his homeland alone. This attitude led to accusations of elitism and recalcitrance against the system. Tarkovsky had little time for Soviet doctrine; as far as he was concerned, he belonged to the nineteenth-century Russian cultural tradition, which was in free creative dialogue with the West. Tarkovsky's 'quotations' are a vital part of this creative dialogue, attempting to eradicate the cultural void that was a consequence of the Soviet regime.[12] At the same time they express his predilection for particular artists, who are an integral part of his personal and creative realm.

Leonardo da Vinci occupies a high place in Tarkovsky's artistic hierarchy. In *Mirror*, the pre-revolutionary album of his paintings and drawings is part of the cultural legacy – both material and genetic – passed on from father to son. We first see Ignat turning its pages in his father's flat. Later in the film, Alexei is looking at the same book, on a table in the woods, shortly before his father appears. Arseni Tarkovsky often spent time with the young Andrei, studying art books. Tarkovsky himself did the same with his second son, Andrei. Art is an organic part of the lives depicted on screen, notwithstanding the difficulties and privations; it provides continuity and refuge, where there is loss and vulnerability. Most importantly for Tarkovsky, it speaks of the eternal and the indestructible in a transient world; it is there like a talisman, warding off the ephemeral, focused on the infinite. Art is also a mirror, which both reflects and interprets, is both surface and depth. Leonardo's portrait of Ginevra de Benci, Tarkovsky tells us, is ambivalent. The woman reflected is at once beautiful and repellent: 'we needed the portrait in order to introduce a timeless element into the moments that are succeeding each other before our eyes, and at the same time to juxtapose the portrait with the heroine, to emphasise in her and the actress the same capacity at once to enchant and to repel.'[13] Indeed, we witness a similarly ambivalent expression on Maria's face, in her reaction to her husband's sudden arrival. Natalia's character pivots around this ambivalence.

Art is present in more oblique ways too: the snow-bound Brueghelian landscape around the shooting range, the red-head's hand shielding the lit branch, her form by the fire, both reminiscent of Georges de la Tour's candlelit canvases. It is echoed also in the poster of Tarkovsky's *Andrei Rublev* inside the narrator's flat. Musically, it embraces the film with some of the most beautiful passages of classical music, transforming what unfolds on the screen. The four poems also work like the music, sublimating and augmenting the actions they accompany. Literary references, too, colour the canvas. In the opening shot, while speaking to the stranger, Maria refers to 'Ward 6', Chekhov's story about a provincial doctor who becomes insane. The stranger, himself a doctor, reassures her that he is not threatened by this and that Chekhov invented it. Later, during the printing-works sequence, Liza attacks Maria through Dostoevsky, comparing her to Maria Lebiadkina. When characters cannot, or will not, speak directly, they have recourse to literature.

Culture and history meet in Pushkin's letter to the Russian philosopher, Piotr Chaadaev, written in 1836. A strange woman and her maid appear in one of the rooms of the narrator's flat; the woman asks Ignat to read her the letter. The woman herself is a cultural and historical reference, and somewhat reminiscent of the poet Anna Akhmatova in her dress and hairstyle, but especially in her profile. Tarkovsky said of her that she was there to unite the severed thread of time. The letter is Pushkin's response to Chaadaev's First Philosophical Letter, in which he ascribed the ills of Russian society to the fact that it had embraced Byzantine Christianity and had thus relinquished the civilising influence of the Catholic Church. As a result of this letter, Chaadaev was declared insane and put under medical surveillance. Its publication, however, sparked off the Westerniser/Slavophile controversy, which has preoccupied Russia ever since. Did Russia have its own, special mission and significance in the world, or was it merely a backward country, doomed to eternal darkness until such time as it would forge closer ties with Europe? Pushkin, Russia's most revered poet, believed that Russia indeed had a distinct historical significance. He pointed out to his friend that it was Russia and its vast expanses that contained the Tartar yoke and saved the Christian world. He assured him that though he was far from pleased at what he saw around him, he would choose no other country and no other history than the one God had given them. This reflects Tarkovsky's own position; his brief sojourn in the West, dictated largely by circumstances rather than by personal choice, ended in nostalgia, disillusionment and premature death.

Pushkin's letter resonates in different ways throughout the film: the landscape around the dacha reveals some of the vast expanses he writes about, which occur again, tormentingly, in the Sivash footage, and in the area around the shooting range. There is a moment of absurdity, too, when the military instructor chides a boy for shooting towards the trees, saying he might accidentally kill someone – a preposterous idea in that empty vastness. The footage of Mao's Cultural Revolution, and the clashes in Damansky Island in 1969, are another reflection of Russia's mission to keep the Mongols con-

11. The Brueghelian landscape surrounding the shooting range, whose vastness is reflected in the Pushkin letter. Asafiev walks up the hill in the foreground. (Photograph: Vladimir Murashko)

tained. Damansky is one of two islands in the Ussuri river that separates China from Russia. An armed conflict ensued in 1969, after Chinese protesters called for the island to be ceded to China. Yet Tarkovsky's choice of footage reveals a certain ambivalence on his part: the Soviet soldiers' features are not far removed from those of the protesters' – more Asiatic than Caucasian; their dull, blunt presence as they stand in the human chain they have created reminds us that they belong to a force as large and as brutal as the millions that hailed the Cultural Revolution. In contrast to this we see many Mongol soldiers in the Sivash footage – Russia here defending itself, and Europe, against the Nazi yoke. Tarkovsky does not merely *show* historical events of his era, he also draws parallels. There is anti-heroism in the Sivash footage, and in the 'liberation' of Prague of 1945. Nor is there anything celebratory about the endless scenes of leave-taking as Spanish children board the ship that will take them to the Soviet Union, and away from their country for ever. And there is an added irony – these children left their war-torn country for a safer place which, a few years later, would be in the throes of another vicious war. Tarkovsky, in his anger at his colleagues' calls for more historical context, had vowed to give them the true life of the nation, and the footage he selected is evidence of that.

An interesting thing to note about the documentary footage is that, unlike the rest of the film, it is presented in chronological order. The Spanish Civil War (1936–39) was a precursor of the terrible war that was to sweep through Europe soon after. Tarkovsky juxtaposes these images of fear, devastation and uprooting with two events from Soviet history of the same period: a record-breaking Soviet ascent to the stratosphere in 1934, and the triumphant welcome given to the aviator Valeri Chkalov, who achieved the first flight over the North Pole to Vancouver Island in 1937. Suddenly, we are in a Brueghelian universe; while in one corner of the historical canvas evil has been unleashed, in another triumphant events are taking place. In the case of the stratosphere balloon, it was a bitter triumph as the three main participants in this ascent perished.[14] In terms of rhythm and texture Tarkovsky again chooses carefully: the Spanish footage is staccato, sharp, confused, erratically moving, propelled by a similar soundtrack; in counterpoint, the huge balloons, resembling the marble folds on the clothes of ancient statues, hover majestically in space. They glide across the frame, triumphantly carrying the name of the USSR, but Pergolesi's music dampens the ideological exultation, instead accentuating their movement and texture, containing their weightlessness. The Chkalov footage is the previous scenes' opposite, both in texture (the frame dense and cluttered with the myriad leaflets falling upon the solemn cars) and in movement (the focus is on the earth, not the sky, and gravity is almost palpable). The next piece of footage we see is the laborious crossing of the Sivash lagoon, which Tarkovsky later said 'had to become the centre, the very essence, heart, nerve of this picture that had started off merely as my intimate lyrical memories'.[15] This footage, which Tarkovsky chanced upon after sifting through hours of familiar footage from that time, signals one of the most important events of Tarkovsky's life: the Second World War.

When asked about his childhood in interview, Tarkovsky replied:

'when people asked me what I dreamed about in childhood, I can say one thing with certainty: we waited for the war to end. I had only two thoughts: I wanted my father to return and the war to end.'[16] War, together with his father's absence, are the formative elements in Tarkovsky's life. In this respect, the director's debut film, *Ivan's Childhood*, was a very precise map of his inner landscape. True childhood was the time before the war; war-time froze the heart, obscured the vision and damaged the child irreparably. *Mirror* provides clear evidence of this: the places and spaces of beauty and harmony belong to the time before the war; from then on, the landscape, inner and outer, changes. War, in its different guises, is there in every one of Tarkovsky's films. In *Mirror*, it is presented as one of the corner-stones of the author's life. We have seen how many of the episodes in the script were devoted to that period. In the film, two episodes (the shooting range and the attempted sale of the earrings), two smaller sequences (the Spaniards and the father's return) and most of the footage reflect different aspects of war. Echoes of war even creep into the present, when the narrator suggests to Natalia that they send Ignat to the Suvorov Military Academy.[17] War both pulls people apart and unites them in loss and grief. The sequence with the Spaniards becomes utterly relevant when looked at in this light; what happened to these people was soon to happen to Tarkovsky and his compatriots. The Spanish immigrants, living among several generations of Soviet citizens, were to be a constant reminder of the tragedy of war.

The Sivash footage is very much a Tarkovskian rendering of war; that is, an expression of both his ethical and aesthetic concerns. When he first came upon it, he was fascinated by the fact that it observed the unity of time, place and action. Here was the same event, filmed from nineteen different angles, by one person. It was also utterly authentic and a far cry from the stock Soviet footage of the war. The sequence was yet another expression of Tarkovsky's search for the Olympian calm of form; it revealed the appalling daily hardships of war with a rare and compelling quietude. For Tarkovsky these were the images of true sacrifice, unrecognised and unknown by most people, who were used to overtly heroic and manipulated war footage. The documentary footage that follows is from the end of the war: cannon fire, the liberation of Prague in 1945, Hitler's corpse (which, as we now know, was a double), the Moscow Victory

Parade of 1945 – which Tarkovsky attended – with Stalin's portrait foregrounded, a still of a man with crutches (a reference to Tarkovsky's father, who had lost his leg in war-time), and the atomic explosion over Hiroshima. The final documentary sequences we see are all from what was then the very near past: the events of 1966–69 in China. All the footage Tarkovsky incorporated into the film was an integral part of his own, and his country's, experience.

Nature and the Elements

> Rain, fire, water, snow, dew, the driving ground wind – all are part of the material setting in which we dwell; I would even say of the truth of our lives.[18]

In his lectures, Tarkovsky told students that they must film not merely nature, but nature *ensouled.* He pointed out that nature requires special preparation during filming, because problems of light, colour and the weather always arise. He was never satisfied with filming a beautiful landscape; in fact, he deliberately avoided beautiful or exotic landscapes, asserting that one must be attentive to every element of nature that will enter a frame. Tarkovsky moved trees, added branches, painted leaves, doing everything in his power to make nature come alive, to reveal the forces that live within it. *Mirror* is the consummate expression of his efforts, a truly pantheistic film. Nature here is not a backdrop, but the protagonist – framing the actors, the author's memories, the child's dreams. The author's imagination, his longing and his dreaming roam the fecund fields, the dense oak forest, the river and the firs that surround the childhood home. The characters do not merely inhabit this landscape; they are immersed in it. Both Tarkovsky and his sister, Marina, have spoken of a childhood that was immersed in nature. Their mother insisted they spend their summer months away from the city, and instilled in them a love and knowledge of the countryside, teaching them the names of trees, flowers and fruits. A long spell in Siberia, on a geological expedition, at the age of twenty-one, also made a lasting impression on Tarkovsky. While there he sketched, painted and observed nature thoroughly, taking in both the microcosm and the macrocosm that he reproduces so effectively in his films.

Nature and the elements are intimately connected with the mother in the film. The first sequence identifies her with the landscape – the field, the forest, the surrounding sounds – and from then on we watch her move with ease about the dacha, although she is quietly preoccupied, sad and apprehensive. The elements of fire and water take soundings of her moods. During the scene of the burning of the shed – a real occurrence, which happened when the Gorchakovs' young son (Vitia in the film) accidentally set fire to their hay shed while playing with matches – Tarkovsky blends rain with fire. In his lectures, he explained that when they first shot the scene there was rain but no fire. When they came to shoot it again, they decided to keep this strange mood created by the presence of rain and fire in the frame, each subject to its own special rhythm and density. The effect is both calming and disturbing, turning this otherwise destructive occurrence into an epiphany, with its redeeming and purifying results. We watch and hear the raindrops quietly falling, and join those present as they stand transfixed by the flames. For Maria it seems like a forewarning of things to come: the fact that her husband will never return. Yet her calm demeanour indicates that she has crossed a threshold, and possibly apprehended something of what awaits her. The fire is both a tragedy and a welcome release. Fire, in a contained form this time – a flame and a burning stove – is indicative of another love: the young Alexei's unrequited love for the red-head, and her own romance with the military instructor. This is a warming, comforting, alluring fire – the fire of the hearth, and the quiet, fragile flame of Alexei's budding desire.

It is important when considering images of the elements in Tarkovsky not to treat them merely as symbols; he rebelled against this narrow interpretation of his use of them, becoming frustrated at recurring questions about the significance of their presence, especially that of water, in his films. He insisted that he merely recorded the truth of the reality he knew; and water – rain, puddles, rivers – was an organic part of that reality and one of the most beautiful. Of water he said:

Certain things are more cinematic, more photogenic than others. Water is very important to me in this respect. It is alive, it has depth, it moves, it changes, it reflects like a mirror, you can drown in it, you can drink it, you can wash yourself. You probably know that the entire mass of water on the earth is made up of one molecule. Water is a monad.[19]

This last idea is particularly important to Tarkovsky, because a monad is another name for God, the divinity that permeates everything, whose ineffable presence he sought to capture through images. Water is also the first mirror, which reflected the sky, the earth and the face of Narcissus. The water-mirror signifies primal awareness, contemplation and vanity, clarity and unification. The French poet Paul Claudel called water 'the gaze of the earth, its instrument for looking at time'.[20] These ideas are part of the fabric and polyphonic quality of *Mirror*. Claudel's phrase would have been music to Tarkovsky's ears, given his concept of the cinema as a sculpture made of time.

On the one hand, water is part of Tarkovsky's formal and aesthetic concerns; his rendering of rhythm, density and texture on the screen. On the other, it creates a mood and an atmosphere which bespeak the heroes' emotions. Maria is usually accompanied by water of some form or other. Her strange ablution, part of the first childhood dream, is simultaneously threatening and a peculiar expression of catharsis. At first, her husband is there, helping her wash her hair in a basin. But soon water begins to run down the walls and rain down from the ceiling, blurring the boundaries between bliss and sorrow, ecstasy and catastrophe, the young woman in the white dress and the old woman – her future self – who comes towards us from the other side of the mirror. The very manifestation of a natural element in a man-made space is disturbing in itself. Tarkovsky offsets this with fire, in the form of a flame burning in a gas stove in a corner of the room. This unusual combination of elements and events on the screen communicates something of Maria's complex emotional state, which is not quantifiable. On the verge of another catastrophe, Maria is drenched by rain as she hastens to the printing works in fear of terrible consequences. When later she seeks an emotional and mental catharsis in the shower, she is let down by the Soviet plumbing system – water will not flow abundantly, to soothe her; it is her tears, another form of water, that will do so. Her humiliating visit to the doctor's house to sell her earrings is offset by rain, in which she and Alexei are callously made to stand by the insensitive doctor's wife. In that same sequence, after Maria has killed the chicken, her disturbing close-up is framed in front of a wall down which water trickles continually. A river witnesses her flight after the aborted sale of the earrings. Water provides flow, movement and catharsis; it is also melancholy and sad. It weeps for Maria when she cannot; it speaks for her turmoil and pain, for her discomfort and vulnerability.

Frozen water, in the form of ice and snow, dominates the episode at the shooting range. On one level, this is a typical Russian winter landscape – a vast, snow-covered expanse of space, an ice-covered river, people on sleds moving about in the snow. Within this landscape is the shooting range, an open-air wooden structure, where we are called to bear witness to the consequences of war through the characters of Asafiev and his shell-shocked military instructor. The landscape is Brueghelian both in form and content. After having observed, in close-up, the quiet tragedy of these two damaged people in the shooting range, the camera tracks out to reveal the winter life unfolding around it, which is unaware of the weeping boy ascending the hill, and the broken military instructor with the tough exterior. The icy, unrelentingly white winter setting and the persistent sound of snow being crushed by heavy boots throughout the sequence are palpable reminders of the frozen, stunted hearts of Asafiev and the instructor – the defiant, indignant orphan and the stuttering, ineffectual grown-up. The huge expanse that surrounds them accentuates their fragility, but also their insignificance, even as their fate reflects the fate of millions in war-time. The Sivash footage, cut into this sequence, parallels this image. Once again people are located in a vast landscape; this time they are laboriously marching through water and mud, carrying heavy artillery. Their efforts are simultaneously futile and heroic: the mud – for Tarkovsky, not mud but 'earth mixed with water, the silt from which things are born'[21] – is both impeding and heroising their progress. Nature surrounds them, disinterested, oblivious; their tragic fate unfolds within it, accentuated by it. At the same time, it has to be remembered that the war was won partly because of this very landscape, whose immensity and harshness proved to be Hitler's nemesis. Its own people have, at the instigation of their rulers, also suffered cruelly because of it. We need only call to mind the millions lost building dams, roads, railways and canals in the Gulag archipelago. These vastly different faces of nature are in counterpoint in *Mirror*. The Pushkin letter reminds us of this most important protagonist of Russia's history, while Tarkovsky illustrates for us its opposing aspects.

If earth, water and fire variously measure effort, time and love, wind embodies the restless, mysterious, disturbing spirit that passes through things. It is the most overt manifestation of animated nature, of nature ensouled, the breath of life and motion. It first occurs in the opening scene, as the stranger is leaving the dacha after his brief meeting with Maria. Tarkovsky wanted to show one final thread between them before the man goes off for ever, but thought that just having him look back at her would be too obvious and artificial. The sudden gust of wind provided the motivation for his action, introducing this unknown, yet familiar, force to the film. The wind, as we have seen, is also connected to the absent father, whose spirit permeates the dacha and the mother's and children's thoughts. In the first dream, it races towards us and the sleeping Alexei from within the forest, alerting him also to the sexual coupling of his parents (he wakes up and sees a white nightdress flung across the adjacent room). A variation of this scene is repeated twice more, the wind this time knocking objects – a loaf of bread, a lamp – off a table left at the edge of the forest. The wind, coupled with rain, chases the boy around the dacha; later it accompanies him into a room filled with white curtains, which it moves through. The wind is also nature's gaze, turned both to the characters and to us, the audience. Because its movement is directed, it addresses us much more starkly than the other elements, though, ironically, it is the only invisible one, unseen, but felt through its effects on the surrounding reality. In this respect, it is the nearest possible embodiment of the divinity, of the spirit of place and of things.

Gaston Bachelard (see note 20) tells us that formal imagination needs the idea of composition, while material imagination needs the idea of combination. Tarkovsky utilises both forms of imagination, but the great power of his films, their unique, palpable textures and rhythms come from his use of the second. The elements are most often used in combination in order to create highly suggestive and unusual 'moods' in nature. The barn fire is dissolved, dissipated, transformed when witnessed in combination with rain; it appears much more potent and dramatic when we see it again, burning, at the centre of the frame, at the edge of the thick forest (Maria's memory in the shower). The sudden gust of wind, which caresses the buckwheat in the beginning of the film, has a different tone and presence from the one which escapes from within the forest and throws the objects off the table, or the one which follows Alexei around the house, accompanied by rain. It is not easy to qualify these differences, to define the mood and atmosphere they communicate, or the diverse emotional responses we may have to them. What is certain is that they engage our sensory, sensual and emotive faculties, inviting us to enter, ponder and observe the world unfolding on the screen; a world whose elements and matter are familiar, yet made strange. Reducing Tarkovsky's use of nature and the elements to symbols and metaphors demeans his vision – one that celebrates the uniqueness and the particular life within each object, phenomenon and sentient being.

Mirror's Chronotopes

The term chronotope (literally time-space, from the Greek *chronos* and *topos*) was given by Mikhail Bakhtin to what he called 'the intrinsic connectedness of temporal and spatial relationships that are artistically expressed in literature'.[22] Though the term can be applied to a range of texts, it is particularly apt for *Mirror*, whose polyphonic nature arises from the diversity and interrelation of its temporal and spatial realities (a vivid example is the merging of time and space in the film's final sequence). For Bakhtin, as for Tarkovsky, time and space are not abstract concepts but forms of the most immediate reality. Tarkovsky represents not only historical time, but time as it lives in each substance, thing and person; he reveals both the passing of time and time as duration. Tarkovsky has the ability to see and read time; in *Mirror*, he captures the *fullness of time*[23] – the inner links between past, present and future. He creates his chronotopes with intent, carefully choosing the site and space that will combine with temporal qualities to communicate his idea. Bakhtin believed that questions about self can be pursued only when treated as specific questions about location. Tarkovsky's chronotopes map an emotional terrain, in as far as we come to apprehend aspects of his characters through their locus. Edited together, the chronotopes reflect and resonate with each other, achieving a meaning and wholeness that *Mirror*'s fragmentary nature might otherwise resist.

Bakhtin tells us that 'every entry into the sphere of meaning is accomplished only through the gates of the chronotope'.[24] In Tarkovsky, meaning evolves not through plot and characterisation, but through a synthesis of nature, objects, structures and people, mediated by a highly personal and psychological feeling for time. These are the raw materials he uses to create his mise-en-scène. Bakhtin suggested that the artist's task is the surmounting of material, that 'everything physical in the material is surmounted precisely as that which is physical'.[25] Each chronotope in the film is created with this in mind; Tarkovsky combines familiar textures, light, objects and spaces in a way that will communicate the essence of each episode. *Mirror*'s first chronotope is the healing of the stutterer. It is neither a memory nor a reconstruction, but a 'documentary', witnessed unmitigated, by Tarkovsky's camera. Yet the mise-en-scène, with the fragile-looking plant, the chair and the uneven wall, on which we can see the shadow of the microphone, are unmistakably Tarkovskian.[26] The boy's final utterance, 'I can speak', is akin to the biblical 'In the beginning was the Word'. It invokes faith, both on the part of the stutterer, who is healed through speech, and of Tarkovsky, who discovers a way to express adequately the things that trouble and excite him.

> Communication always demands exertion. Without it, indeed without passionate commitment, it is actually not possible for one person to understand another. And so the discovery of a method becomes the discovery of someone who has acquired the gift of speech. And at that point we speak of the birth of an image; that is, of a revelation [...] The limp word, 'search', clearly does not apply to the triumph over a muteness that demands unrelieved, superhuman effort.[27]

These comments and the scene itself are an apt illustration of the surmounting of material.

The film's predominant chronotope, that of the childhood home, is a creative synthesis of several early childhood 'homes'. Tarkovsky was born in Zavrazhe, on the north bank of the Volga, 360 km north-east of Moscow, in a house that belonged to his maternal grandmother's second husband, Nikolai Petrov. He was the doctor who delivered him, 'right on the dinner table covered with a starched

white table-cloth', as the narrator tells us. The house stood in the
lower part of Zavrazhe, which was buried under the waters of the
Volga when a hydroelectric dam was built in the area in 1950.
Tarkovsky also spent several summers in the village of Iurievets,
opposite Zavrazhe, on the south side of the Volga, where his grand-
parents moved in the year following his birth. He was evacuated
there, with his mother and sister, between 1941 and 1943. The dacha
re-created in *Mirror*, as we know, was owned by the Gorchakov family
and located near Ignatievo, 80 km west of Moscow. Tarkovsky spent
the summers of 1935–37 there. Under a decree by Stalin to move
free-standing dachas to the nearest villages, the house was moved to
the village of Ignatievo in 1940; that was to be the Tarkovskys' last
summer there.

Tarkovsky chose to make the Gorchakovs' house the stable child-

12. The Gorchakovs' dacha that embodied the concept of home for
Tarkovsky. The dacha built for *Mirror* was based on this photograph.
(Photograph: Lev Gornung)

hood home he had never known. Perhaps it was because his parents had still not separated in those early years, and he remembered something of their life together there. He also chose to imagine the early days of their love, and even his conception, at the dacha. At the end of the film, the young parents are lying in a field near the house, and the father asks Maria whether she wants a boy or a girl. In the memory sequences, the interiors of the dacha are bathed in a rich golden light. The predominant element is wood: the walls are made of large logs, the floors of wide wooden beams. The furniture is wooden, simple and rough, as befits a dacha. There are kerosene lamps and flowers everywhere, in glass vases, or in thick bunches on the tables. Farm equipment hangs on the walls; large glass jars are filled with water and milk. Outside, on a bench, a basin gathers water; it looks identical to the one the mother will wash her hair in, in the dream sequence. There are objects on the tables and window-sills: a burning candle, books, eggs, potatoes, bread, bowls of raspberries in milk and sugar that the children eat out of. Everything is simple, organic and harmonious in that space. The objects look as though they have always belonged there; the space is lived in, beloved and familiar. The camera records the surrounding objects almost tenderly, as though caressing them. It lingers, as if attempting to empathise with them, to 'hear' them, to reveal their secret life. The adult narrator returns repeatedly to this charmed, idealised realm of childhood 'where everything is still possible, everything is still ahead'.

The chronotopes of the dreams/visions that appear to be taking place within the space of the dacha, are different from those of the memories and sound a disturbing, disquieting note. First, they are all filmed in monochrome and mostly in slow motion. Secondly, because they are displaced to the interior plane, they possess certain elements that allow for the strangeness and dislocation we experience in dreams. The room young Alexei is sleeping in does not resemble any in the dacha; it is more richly decorated and cluttered. The adjacent room, glimpsed briefly, is similarly decorated; but what follows it, during the ablution sequence with the mother, is a space which, judging by its arched windows, could be a room in the narrator's Moscow flat. Although we might assume that the dream is taking place at the dacha (the first shot is the recurring one of the wind blowing out of the forest) none of its spaces can be identified with

13. This interior of the Gorchakovs' dacha, taken in 1935, closely resembles that created by Tarkovsky in *Mirror*. (Photograph: Lev Gornung)

it. Another dream/vision, which also takes place in a non-identifiable space, is Maria's levitation. The room is bare, save for an iron bed. Maria, lying on her side, is suspended several feet above it, the long cord of her night-dress hanging, like a strange umbilical cord. This flight motif, found also in *Solaris* and *The Sacrifice*, is an image of sexual love. In *Mirror* the scene begins with Maria's husband stroking her hand; yet, when we see her fully, she is alone in her flight, as she is in her love.

The last two dreams are clearly located at the dacha, but they have an eerie, disturbing quality. In one, the dacha itself, surrounded with pine trees, appears alive, with its lit windows like eyes staring out of its dark face. A chicken escapes out of one of the windows, breaking through the glass. Young Alexei runs towards the house, chased by the wind. He is looking for his mother, but cannot open the wooden door to the shed where she might be. The door opens by itself as soon as he leaves, to reveal her calmly gathering potatoes. There is an element of cruelty and menace in this dream. The boy is taking flight from some unknown power, personified by the wind. But he cannot find shelter and comfort with his mother, he cannot enter the place she is in. In fact, young Alexei is alone, or kept on an uncomfortable threshold, in all the dreams. In the last dream, he opens a door and runs into the darkness of what looks like a room in the dacha, filled with lace curtains and tablecloths hanging up to dry. Behind them is a mirror, inside which we catch his reflection holding a large jar filled with milk, which he brings up to his lips. The wind is blowing through this room too, and the boy is alone, inside this strangely animated inanimate world. The space of the dreams does not have the warm, comforting glow of the space of the memories; it reveals an unconscious which is at odds with the fond memories of childhood Tarkovsky sought to recapture.

Another dacha, the rich doctor's, where Maria goes to sell her earrings in war-time, is very different in atmosphere from the childhood home. Though it, too, is made of wood, it appears heavy and dark, as no natural daylight comes in through the windows. The furniture is voluminous and formal; instead of books, there are glass cabinets filled with porcelain cups. The spilt milk, which was part of the pre-war idyll of the Gorchakovs' dacha, is an insult here at a time when so many people across the country were dying of starvation. Everything in this house is an insult, a slap across Maria's face: the woman's luxurious dress, her child's embarrassingly lush bed, the elaborate kerosene lamps, the maid who washes the floors, the callousness with which the woman suggests Alexei should kill the chicken, since Maria refuses. Soviet audiences, for whom the war remained an open wound, would have quickly read the signs and noted the significance of this episode. Such luxury and plenty in war-time is hubris – the chronotope of this house is at odds with the nation's. In the film, Maria takes flight, disgusted, unable to sell her earrings. Tarkovsky's own mother did sell her turquoise earrings, family heirlooms that her husband loved. One day she went off across the Volga with them and returned with a bucketful of potatoes.

The deprivations of war-time are better captured in an interior briefly glimpsed in the sequence of the father's sudden return from the front, which was filmed at the dacha of the writer Bruno Iasensky, in Peredelkino. Maria had gone there with her children in the summer of 1943 to work as a janitor at a children's camp. Arseni Tarkovsky appeared on an unexpected visit from the front that summer. The next time they saw him was at the end of that year; by then, his leg had been amputated and he walked on crutches. In the scene, what we see of the house looks decrepit and empty. Maria is crouching on a rough wooden floor, across which pieces of furniture are strewn, trying to cut up bits of wood, presumably to light a fire. Outside, Alexei is looking at the Leonardo book. His sister says, 'I'll tell them you stole the book'. This scene alludes to a time when the young Tarkovsky came across some old books at the dacha of the well-known war poet Vera Inber, in Peredelkino. He cut out pictures from them in order to add to his paper army, with which he played at war with the other boys. In the film, this episode is sublimated to the Leonardo volume and to the theme of personal and historical legacies.

The narrator's flat, various parts of which are seen throughout the film, apparently became an attraction of sorts at Mosfilm, and people would go on 'excursions' to see it.[28] It was re-created in one of the large studios there, and reportedly had almost all the props-people of Mosfilm working on it. It is made to resemble an old Moscow flat, containing remnants of time past: a tiled stove, cast-iron radiators, an old bathtub on legs and rusting, leaking pipes. It consists of a long corridor, with a series of rooms giving off it, but the way it is filmed makes it feel like a rambling, labyrinthine structure, where the individual spaces appear to change their positions constantly. Everywhere there are half-opened doors. One of the rooms is disused, with peeling wallpaper; it is here that the two women appear to Ignat. Another room, glimpsed fleetingly, appears to be overflowing with books. Where there is furniture, it is formal and heavy, often carved and made of dark wood; there are high-backed chairs, large tables, a stand, a wooden screen. The taste is refined, and reminiscent of the rich doctor's dacha. There are none of the stock Soviet cabinets, libraries and cupboards, which are part and parcel of most Russian flats. A French poster of *Andrei Rublev* and photographs of Tarkovsky's parents on the walls leave us in no doubt as to the identity of the occupant. The flat is filled with textures: darkly painted walls, tiles, copper sheets, glass bricks, polished floors, old, torn wallpaper, splitting plaster, lace, glass jars with flowers, and many mirrors of varying sizes in thick wooden frames. The atmosphere here is austere, weighed down, cold. It is mostly a place of conflicts and arguments, of painful memories and an impending death. As important as the interiors are the exteriors to the flat. Through the large windows, we catch glimpses of the run-down corridor outside the front door, and the courtyard, where Ignat is later seen stoking the bonfire he has made. These 'exterior' spaces in some ways better capture the chronotope of the present than the flat does, with its timeless, old-world quality, its emptiness and its ghosts.

An important historical chronotope, Stalin's Terror, is re-created in the printing-works sequence. The location is apt, considering the importance of literary propaganda in the Soviet State. Tarkovsky's mother worked as a proof-reader all her life, at the First Obraztsovo printing works, located near their Moscow flat. The events described did not happen to her but to another proof-reader who was fired for making a mistake, even though it was corrected while still in the proofs. Her fate could have been much worse, since mistakes in official publications were considered political crimes during Stalin's reign. The sequence is filmed mostly in black and white with some monochrome shots. It is dominated by rows of desks, large, black, rhythmic presses and long, mostly empty, white corridors. Unnaturally shining light bulbs, resembling interrogation lamps, fill the various rooms. The heavy, metallic, mechanical presence of the presses is offset by the plants – a fixture of every Soviet workplace – filling the window-sills and hanging from the ceiling. On the walls are posters with slogans of the time and, more disturbingly, portraits of two of the most feared men of the system, Felix Dzerzhinsky, the notorious head of the Cheka from 1919 until his death in 1926, and Stalin himself. The camera does not linger on these portraits, but it registers them as it tracks through the spaces, following the mother's nervous movements through endless corridors strewn with large rolls of paper, in search of the proofs. The imperceptible slow-motion used in these scenes retards her movement, thus prolonging her mute fear and sense of urgency, making them more palpable. This sequence is a glittering example of the 'Olympian calm of form'. Everything is understated, internalised, until Liza's sudden eruption, which provides an outlet for the tension the two women have experienced in this

14. Tarkovsky's sister, Marina, remembers him studying this photograph very intently. It is a double exposure depicting Marina, her son Misha and her mother Maria, and was taken in Ignatievo in 1962 by Marina's husband. Its embodiment of the simultaneity of time and the coexistence of parallel worlds may have inspired the film's final sequence, both formally and thematically. (Photograph: Alexander Gordon)

potentially life-threatening situation. Tarkovsky communicates everything through the soundtrack, the mise-en-scène, the terse dialogue and the camera movements.

The concluding sequence of *Mirror* is the most poignant illustration of the fullness of time. Set in the landscape around the dacha and unravelling to Bach's St John Passion, it is a remarkable tour-de-force, celebrating nature and roots, the fruits of love, and the cycles of life. We see the dacha and, in the field before it, Maria and her husband, in the early days of their love, discussing their future children. Then we see the old woman with the boy Alexei. Then the camera tracks across time to what are the rotting remains of the foundations of the dacha, and the well Maria once drank water from, now filled with debris. White sheets are drying on old wooden beams; the old mother leaves the basin of clothes she has been carrying and leads her children across the familiar landscape, while her young self watches them all from across the field. This unity of place in the life of the generations is what Bakhtin calls the idyllic chronotope, a special corner of the world in which ancestors lived and where their children will live. Here the temporal boundaries between individual lives, and within a single life, are made less distinct, thus revealing the cyclical nature of time. The basic realities of life, including sexuality, are presented in a sublimated form and, most importantly, the life of nature is merged with human life, observing a common rhythm and language. Tarkovsky concludes *Mirror* with this small corner of eternity, situated outside the forces of history and human progress. It is the final resting-place of Alexei's soul.

Tarkovsky's Characters

Tarkovsky's characters can best be described as states of being, states of mind and soul. They do not have developing, evolving personalities. We come upon them at a specific moment in time, in a state of deep spiritual crisis and tension. To a certain degree, they are extensions of the director's own concerns and conflicts, not sufficiently independent from him to lead an autonomous life on the screen. For Tarkovsky, the most interesting characters are outwardly static while inwardly burning with an overriding passion. He has spoken of his predilection for characters who cannot adapt themselves to life pragmatically, who feel a moral imperative and possess an inner freedom which compels them to act in their own, unique way. The questions Tarkovsky asks through them are always the same: what is the meaning of our lives, what is our duty, what is our relationship to others, to the world, to ourselves? What are the emotions that assail us? In *Mirror*, every frame contains one of these questions, every image hints, obliquely, at a possible answer. And every image hovers between opposite poles. Lightness comes with longing, not with happiness; achievement comes with death; fear is attached to elegance and defiance. People are mute, and in their muteness their feelings become even more powerful, because they permeate every aspect of their being. Through treating his characters as archetypes and ciphers, Tarkovsky achieves a distillation of the fundamental emotions: loss, fear, longing, love, desire and sacrifice.

Unlike Tarkovsky's other films, which are centred around one, or more, male heroes, *Mirror* is largely centred around women and children. The male characters – the author and his father excepted – are secondary. The strange doctor of the opening scene was introduced to show Maria's cool unavailability and longing for her absent husband, but also because Tarkovsky wanted to include his beloved actor, Anatoli Solonitsyn. He breezes through the scene with a light and sardonic manner, delightfully eccentric and affecting, though ultimately failing to 'thaw' Maria. Another Tarkovsky favourite, Nikolai Grinko, appears briefly as Maria's fatherly, comforting boss at the printing works. The military instructor is a more substantial part. He is the young Alexei's rival for the affections of the red-head, a man traumatised by war (his nickname is Shell-shock); he speaks tersely, stutters, is unemotional and at times even cruel, but – as he demonstrates by throwing himself on the hand grenade – ultimately willing to sacrifice himself for others. The secondary female characters – Liza and Nadezhda Petrovna, the rich doctor's wife – serve primarily to foreground aspects of Maria's emotional states. The two women in Alexei's flat are ciphers for a cultural past. Significantly, they, and not his immediate family, are the incredulous witnesses to his impending death. Tellingly, the doctor in this scene is played by Misharin who, as Tarkovsky's co-author and friend, emerges as a 'confessor' and a catalyst of his ideas. He is credited with understanding the true nature of Alexei's malady – conscience and memory.

Author and Hero

While on the set of *Mirror*, Tarkovsky, speaking to the film critic Olga Surkova, explained what he was attempting with his latest film: 'I don't want to screen a subject, even one filtered through my own perception, but to make my own memory, my attitudes, my comprehension or incomprehension of something, my condition, in the end, into the subject of the film.'[29] In other words, Tarkovsky wanted to take an imprint of his inner territory at 24 frames a second. He went on to say that he wanted to bring into being through the film – in a philosophical, rather than in an aesthetic sense – the moral principle in art and in life, in the relationship between art and life. In the film, as narrator, he addresses this point explicitly when Alexei tells Natalia that 'a book is neither an invention nor a source of income, but a deed! A poet is called to stir the soul profoundly, not to cultivate idol-worshippers!' *Mirror* was to become a purifying moral deed, a confession, which might lead to absolution. This entails taking responsibility for one's life and the expression of that life – in Tarkovsky's case through art. And so the artist Tarkovsky speaks about the world and emotions of Tarkovsky the child and Tarkovsky the man; the relationship between author and hero here becomes the relationship between the artist and the human being. Bakhtin tells us that the relationship between art and life can be achieved only through the unity of answerability: 'I have to answer with my own life for what I have experienced and understood in art, so that everything I have experienced and understood would not remain ineffectual in my life.'[30] Tarkovsky could not be more in accord with this idea for, in the end, it can be argued that he did answer with his own life for what he had come to understand through his art. His films changed his life, partly through the consequences he suffered for making them in a monolithic and punishing system, and partly because through them he was able to tap into deeper truths about himself, which in the end became fatally prophetic.

Answerability, Bakhtin tells us, entails guilt and liability for blame. While Tarkovsky has always put aspects of himself into the heroes of his films, in *Mirror*, for the first time, he personalises the author, by placing around him the objects of his, Tarkovsky's, guilt: his mother and father, his first wife and son. If in *Andrei Rublev* he dealt with the theme of the artist's responsibility to his time and his people, to his God and to himself, in *Mirror* he addresses the artist's human dimension, and his answerability to each and every one of those closest to him. It has to be remembered that the hero of *Mirror* was conceived during the time of *Andrei Rublev*. In *Solaris*, which followed it, Tarkovsky planted the seeds of the themes of memory and guilt, childhood and family. This thematic 'leak' into a science-fiction film is revealing of Tarkovsky's deeper preoccupations and frame of mind at the time. Tracing Tarkovsky's alter egos through his film heroes we see the stunted child Andrei/Ivan transformed into the artist Tarkovsky/Rublev and pass through a confused Andrei/Kris searching for answers in a dissociated realm, before attempting a return to the earth and to the human family as Andrei/Alexei in *Mirror*. This progression is inevitable for Tarkovsky as artist and as man. For Tarkovsky the artist, it culminates in a work of unique form and meaning. For Tarkovsky the man, it proves fatal and irreversible.

Tarkovsky's partiality for the Olympian calm of form was not merely a theoretical and aesthetic position arrived at through intellectual rigour; it was also a result of his own human limitations, his inability to express emotion directly, to be open, receptive and expansive towards those who really mattered in his life. In his diary of 1970, he writes about this difficulty and his fraught relationship with his family – of the shyness between himself and his parents, of the tortured, unspoken, complicated love they bear each other. He admits that he cannot express his love towards them and finds it easier to relate to strangers, but suspects that this inability to communicate directly is something inherited from his father's side of the family. Whatever the case, this emotional disability is subordinated, or sublimated, into a 'calm of form', which necessarily transformed the truths of life into the stuff of art. Some of the facts are there: Tarkovsky's father had left him and his mother, and he, in turn, left his first wife and son. Both women never remarried, remaining devoted to their children and their husbands. Tellingly, Tarkovsky left his second family out of the film, though both his second wife and his step-daughter have parts in it – the rich doctor's wife and the red-head, respectively. Tarkovsky's autobiography, then, is not an unmediated confession but a highly selective ordering of the material of his life.

Tarkovsky as author is the bearer of form of the film. He breathes life into the organism he has created, he chooses and determines its rhythm, its movements, its utterances, its silences; he gathers it up in his unifying consciousness. However close he may come to the hero, the invisible narrator, the very act of creation will put distance between them. Tarkovsky the hero will be fragmented, distilled and subjugated by Tarkovsky the author. At the same time, Tarkovsky the hero, for all his autobiographical connection to his author, will become a distinct *other*, for the audience and, ultimately, for his author. Autobiography, like biography, is also based on conjecture, embellishment, intuition and invention. As Tarkovsky groped for meaning and expression, he constantly modified the form the film was going to take. Even when filming was over, he continued, even more vigorously, to modify the form. One of the consequences of this was that the off-screen narrator's role grew, resulting partly, as we have noted, from the constant calls for more clarity, and also because his excitement over Terekhova brought about additional scenes, inspired by his own marital conflict. Tarkovsky left his first wife, Irma Raush, and son, Arseni, in the mid-1960s, when he met Larisa Kizilova; by the time of the making of *Mirror*, he had married her and fathered a second son. However, he went through five years of guilt and indecision, some aspects of which are revealed in the scenes between Natalia and Alexei. But here, too, comparisons are not straightforward, since Tarkovsky transfers some of his experience from his own parents' break-up into the lives of these two characters.

The long search for a title for the film indicates the changing relationship between the director and his work and reveals the process of solving questions of form. *Confession*, the earliest title, identifies Tarkovsky, the author, with the work, eradicating all distance between them. Confession happens in the first person singular, is rooted in guilt and entails absolution. The second title, *A White Day*, unites the director Tarkovsky with the poet Tarkovsky. Son identifies with Father, and the hero combines in himself the dual consciousness of the son and the father, something he does indeed do in the film. But the title in itself is more abstract; it suggests a story, which might take place in the whiteness of snow, or in the whiteness of a very bright light. It becomes a poetic metaphor for content, thus introducing distance between the author and the work. Some of the other titles Tarkovsky noted down also maintain this distance, but introduce an element of threat and disturbance: *The Raging Stream* and *The Rapacious Hare* do not sit well with the Olympian calm of form. They are too defined, mobile and expressive as titles, not abstract enough; paradoxically they become too abstract and hermetic when juxtaposed with the content of the film. Another title Tarkovsky was keen on at one time was *Why are you standing so far away?* It carries a private significance: there is one other person involved, whom the author directly addresses. The title somehow implies a woman; but is it the mother, the wife, the father? The latter seems more probable but here again the title is too narrow and specific for the content of the film. Tarkovsky noted two more titles in his diary, both directly identified with him as author: *Redemption*, as a desired outcome of the act of confession, and *Martyrology* (the history of Christian martyrs), with its obviously religious connotation, which becomes self-indulgent when applied to Tarkovsky himself.

Mirror, the title Tarkovsky finally chose, is perfectly apt – both semantically and metaphorically – for the content of the film, but also in telling us something about Tarkovsky's position in relation to it. Alexander Misharin said that Tarkovsky decided on 'mirror' because he was fascinated by how it looked when written down: ЗЕРКАЛО [zerkalo]. His sight was captivated by a word whose semantic roots – зреть [zret'], зеркать [zerkat'], зоркий [zorkii], эрение [zrenie] – imply not merely looking, but beholding, gazing, looking vigilantly, intently, perspicaciously at something. The verb *zret* (declined differently) also means to ripen, to mature. Therefore the word itself reveals a *way* of looking and, by aural association, a process of maturing, ripening. We might recall a key scene in the film in which Alexei, waiting for his mother, looks at his image in the mirror in the doctor's house. It is as if he is seeing himself for the first time. And we the audience (*zriteli*, from the same root) also see him for the first time; his face in the mirror somehow looks different from the face we have seen thus far on the screen. It might be the angle, the quality of light and shadow, or even the surrounding reality; the music which accompanies the scene also hints at the uniqueness of this moment of awareness and transformation that is noted by audience, author and character.

Bakhtin tells us that 'we evaluate our exterior not for ourselves, but *for* others *through* others'. This is a response to – and an argument against – those who were quick to accuse Tarkovsky of narcissism and lack of modesty; the act of intense looking never happens in a void, but always in dialogue. And its results will always be a surprise and, ultimately, a gift and a legacy to others. Mirrors, after all, signify relationships; they are never vacant, in limbo, but always engaged, reflecting (and distorting) the formal reality of the visible world. Alexei looks in the mirror, but then the shot is reversed, and the mirror gazes at him, producing a slightly different image of him. The mirror reproduces images, but also contains and absorbs them, retaining its interest in them. It is an instrument of self-contemplation but also serves as a door into a different reality. These themes are all present in a film that was a deed and an act of accountability from a man for whom the ability to 'speak' was not inherent but, as the prologue tells us, the result of an act of will, concentration and faith. In his diary of 1982, eight years after the making of *Mirror*, Tarkovsky quoted the epigraph from Herman Hesse's novel *Damien* saying it could just as well be the epigraph to *Mirror*. In it he saw the explanation of the scene with the stutterer. 'Mine is not a pleasant story, it does not possess the gentle harmony of invented tales; like the lives of all men who have given up trying to deceive themselves, it is a mixture of nonsense and chaos, madness and dreams [...] All I wanted was to tempt into life things that wanted to come out of me. Why was it so hard?'[31]

Fathers and Sons

Ostensibly a film about Tarkovsky's mother, *Mirror* is in fact a film truly about fathers and sons, since the first and most important person Tarkovsky employs to speak with him – recognising in him the same authorial powers as in himself – is his father, the poet Arseni Tarkovsky. He does this by including his father's poetry as part of the voice-over that accompanies the images. The father, like the hero, lives mostly outside the frame (we see him briefly four times) yet his absence permeates the screen; the young narrator dreams of him, waking up in the night calling his name; the wind invokes his spirit; the woman sitting on the fence waits for him, but a stranger comes – father is never coming back. Later, during the telephone conversation between Alexei and his mother, we are told that father had left them in 1935. In fact Arseni left his family in 1937. Andrei followed in his father's footsteps, officially divorcing from his first wife in 1970, marrying his second wife that same year, after their son, Andrei, was born. 'Live in the house and the house will stand', Arseni Tarkovsky admonishes us in the poem *Life, Life*, recited in the film. In life it proved an impossible task for both men; they could live effectively only in the metaphorical house of art and human culture. The house of family was not the one where they felt most at home,

15 and 16. Tarkovsky father and son posing before the same mirrored wardrobe. Arseni seen here in 1937, Andrei in 1948, on his sixteenth birthday. (Photographs: Lev Gornung)

though Tarkovsky carried within himself a life-long nostalgia for an idealised family and home.

In the film Tarkovsky addresses his own relationship with his first son, also called Arseni, through the figure of the hero's son, Ignat. He also merges Ignat with the hero, Alexei, as an adolescent, by having both played by the same actor. And he transfers some of his own experience during his parents' separation to that of his son Arseni/Ignat. In the film, Alexei asks his estranged wife, Natalia, to let Ignat come to live with him. Tarkovsky in conversation with his friend and collaborator on *Nostalgia*, Tonino Guerra, said that one night he had overheard his father ask his mother to let him go and live with him. The young Tarkovsky lay in bed for a long while wondering how he would respond if his parents had wanted to discuss this question with him. 'I understood then that I would never have gone to live with my father, even though it was something I always dreamed about, for I suffered over not living with him. But I would never have gone to live with him.'[32] In the film Tarkovsky re-creates this imaginary conversation, which in his own life never took place, between the hero and his son, and gives him his own unvoiced response, here a swift, astonished 'No, it isn't necessary'.

Tarkovsky does not re-create his own relationship with his father in any way; all we sense is the young child's longing for the absent father, and the desperation and sorrow with which he clings to him in the only scene in the entire film where they actually meet. Father appears suddenly, in uniform, on furlough, taking his wife and children by surprise. Interestingly, he calls out only his daughter, Marina's, name, but the young Alexei races over to him as fast as he can, stumbling and falling with the effort. Tears run down his confused face as he presses himself to his father's body, while over by the trees lies open the book of Leonardo drawings that Alexei's own son, Ignat, will leaf through several decades later. In the film this 'future' scene happens earlier, one of the devices Tarkovsky uses throughout to communicate the indivisibility of time, the fact that 'the future is accomplished here and now' and the notion that there is 'one table for great-grandfather and grandson',[33] both instances of a merging of the artistic and emotional consciousness of Arseni and Andrei Tarkovsky. Tarkovsky said that his father influenced him on a genetic, unconscious level; and throughout his life he was sharply aware of his father's artistic consciousness as the true sphere of their relationship.

This salutary merging does not take place between Alexei and Ignat in the film, even though Natalia complains to Alexei that she has noticed 'with horror' how Ignat is becoming more like him. The relationship between this father and son is fraught with unease and clumsiness. Alexei appears to be embarrassed by Ignat; he berates him to Natalia, calls him a block-head, criticises his school results, and the way she is bringing him up. Even though he invites Ignat to live with him, we learn from Natalia, who chides him on this point, that he sees him rarely. At Ignat's first visit to his flat he scolds him over a triviality, then later seems to be absent, and attempts, rather ineffectively, a friendly chat with him over the phone, in which he tells him of his love for the red-head. Yet, while Tarkovsky/Alexei the man is not an inspired or natural communicator, Tarkovsky the author

17. Three generations of Tarkovskys. From left: Arseni, Tarkovsky's first son, his father the poet Arseni, and Tarkovsky himself, 1981. (Photograph: Georgi Binkhasov)

bestows his artist's legacy and care upon the young Ignat through the strange visitation involving the two women. This 'historical memory' is a quiet gift to the boy of his historical and cultural roots. These roots are called upon to replace the absent father; they seem to be the only thing that he is able actively to give his son. This echoes Tarkovsky's father's own gift to his son, the difference being that the director used this gift and forged his own artistic consciousness. In life, Tarkovsky's elder son rejected it. Alexei's fraught relationship with Ignat in the film is perfectly echoed in life by Tarkovsky's difficulties with his first-born, Arseni, with whom he was able to achieve only a modicum of connectedness. The real object of his love was his son from his second marriage, Andrei, whom, in an ironic twist of fate he, unwillingly, also 'left' for four years when deciding to remain in the West; the Soviet authorities would not let his son join him, hoping this might bring Tarkovsky back. It did not.

Mothers and Wives

'I have always said that you look like my mother', Alexei tells Natalia while she looks at herself in the mirror. She responds that this is probably the reason for their separation. He adds that every time he remembers his childhood and his mother, she always has Natalia's face. He explains that this is because he feels pity for them both, but does not respond to Natalia's question as to why he feels this pity. As with the actor for the adolescent father and son, Tarkovsky has his leading actress, Margarita Terekhova, play both mother and wife. As we know from the archives, this was a decision arrived at jointly by Tarkovsky and the Creative Unit, who were very impressed by her acting skills. It was an opportune decision, since Tarkovsky had finally realised that the interview idea would not work, yet still wanted to weave the present into the fabric of the film. Interestingly, Tarkovsky did not want Terekhova to alter her pitch significantly in playing the two parts. As Natalia, she is more extrovert, ironic and vain. As Maria, everything is focused inwards; she is dignified, reserved and contemplative. Natalia wears her hair down, whereas Maria's is always in a plaited bun, except for the scenes with her husband at the end of the film, where she is still a young wife, contemplating her future children.

Throughout Tarkovsky's work, the sexual realm has always been sublimated to the familial. In *Solaris* the mother and wife merge in the hero's consciousness by appearing in the same clothes. In *The Sacrifice* the lover/witch, Maria, also appears in the wife's clothes. In *Nostalgia* Eugenia, the Russian protagonist's translator and possible lover, is shown consoling his wife. Nowhere in Tarkovsky's films is the sensual/sexual element of the female allowed to connect directly with that of the hero. In *Mirror*, this fusion has become one of the film's formal elements; Tarkovsky holds up a mirror to the feminine and the image that he sees in it is that of the wife/mother. Of course the images of these two outwardly identical women are qualitatively different. Each carries a different weight and meaning by virtue of the physical reality the director surrounds her with. Both share a certain reserve and abruptness with regard to their children. But

18. A photograph of Terekhova and Maria Tarkovskaia taken on set, and later used in one of the scenes in *Mirror*. (Photograph: Vladimir Murashko)

whereas Natalia is always shown in discord – with Alexei, with her son, even with herself – Maria is idealised, almost beatified. She possesses a mute integrity, doubtless carved out by suffering and loss; her loneliness is painfully palpable at times; but we know, we see, that she has also been blessed by love.

Unlike Maria, Natalia does not have a realm of her own. We always encounter her in Alexei's flat. While there, she spends most of her time looking at herself in one of his numerous mirrors, and speaking to him through them. She is tense and brittle, as reflected in the conversations between them. They bicker over their son, Ignat, and she chides him over the way he treats his mother. Her knowledge of his mother's whereabouts and condition indicates that she has a close relationship with her. She identifies with his mother and her plight, being herself in a similar situation; she speaks for her, defends her and urges Alexei to reconcile himself to her. Tarkovsky as Alexei reveals hostility towards both women. He urges Natalia to marry, so that Ignat does not have to suffer the negative results of growing up with women as he did. Tarkovsky often mentioned growing up surrounded by women, and of how he missed his father. Yet he said that he was indebted to his mother for everything, because she helped him to realise himself, in the face of terrible adversity and poverty. While Tarkovsky as Alexei reveals an animosity and hostility towards both the mother and wife, Tarkovsky as author bestows upon the figure of the mother a love and grace, which he does not cede to that of the wife. Tellingly, in a later scene, where Natalia is looking at photographs of herself and the mother, wondering at how alike they really are, Alexei – closer to his authorial self here – rejects his earlier claim of their uncanny resemblance. In reality, Irma Raush did indeed resemble the young Maria Vishniakova, and the two remained close even after Tarkovsky had left Raush.

When we first encounter the mother she is sitting on a wooden fence, the boundary of her realm – the beloved, idealised dacha of Tarkovsky's childhood. The camera treats her with a sense of awe and wonder, moving about her as about a precious, treasured object; it circles her lovingly, taking in her still form from many angles, turning her into a sculpture. She is luminous; her skin's whiteness is accentuated by the black jersey she wears, her whole being shines forth

19. (left) Maria Tarkovskaia in Zavrazhe, 1932.

20. (below) Tarkovsky reconstructed the image with Terekhova in the film's opening shots. (Photographs: Lev Gornung; Vladimir Murashko)

from the dark green background of the cluster of trees that enfold the wooden house. Inside the house, she is luminous again, as she walks through its faintly lit rooms, or sits quietly in its dark corners. She is both still and mobile – the centre and hearth of the house, but also searching and restless with some secret knowledge. Her realm speaks of sorrow, longing and a failing hope; she is waiting for someone who, we come to realise, will never return. She is somewhat like the mythical Eyrydice, wrenched away from her beloved, the poet Orpheus. In the myth, Death took Eyrydice and Orpheus went to seek her in the Underworld to bring her back. But when he turned round to see if she was following him – something he had been cautioned against – he lost her to Hades for ever. Maria has been abandoned by her Orpheus, also a poet; frozen in time, she waits for him to return for her. He does not return, however; instead, a stranger engages her attention for a while. But his spirit is with her through his poetry, which tells of the love that once was – a love that took flesh through their two children – and which still fills her heart. Tarkovsky told his friend Tonino Guerra that he remembered well how his mother waited for his father to return from the city, and that he wanted to include this episode in *Mirror*. In reality, there was no meeting with a doctor, but with some artists from the neighbouring village, attempting to talk to his mother, making hints that were no sooner voiced than quashed. In the film, he chooses to show his mother's deep preoccupation and expectation by inventing the episode with the doctor. There is no place in her life for anyone else's existence, and she is aloof and almost hostile during the meeting, obviously uninterested in communicating.

The figure of Maria is the resonator of several realities Tarkovsky wished to examine. On one level, she carries within her being the continuity of time and – by virtue of the fact that she is the bearer of children – of the race. When we first see her she is a young mother, surrounded by the beauty and harmony of nature and the house. Yet disturbing notes creep in almost immediately; the idyll of nature is interrupted by the barn fire, to which she reacts with the same stoic acceptance and reserve we will witness in later episodes. This small tragedy in the heart of beauty reveals the tone and the form Tarkovsky uses to speak of the small tragedies that are part of every episode in the film; the fire does not run amok, but it *does* destroy the barn.

21. Maria with Andrei at the Gorchakovs' dacha, 1935, looking on at the half-built shed, which was later to succumb to fire. (Photograph: Lev Gornung)

Equally, throughout the film, people do not have dramatic breakdowns, but there is always some detail, or some oblique reference, which reveals to us the wounds and the infection in their psyches.

The first poem we hear immediately envelops Maria in profound romantic love and secret sorrow. But the dream sequence that follows introduces a disturbing twist on what, on the face of it, is an act of intimacy and affection: a man washing a woman's hair. As she stands in her white dress, hair wet, arms hanging, like a strange human scarecrow (her boss calls her that in the printing-works sequence), water runs down the walls, the ceiling plaster begins to fall and an everyday act is transformed. A dissonant – if poetic – space is created, which we watch her glide through, as though undisturbed, yet knowing; she confronts her own fate when she sees in the mirror the old woman she will become, walking towards her.

In his original proposal for the film, Tarkovsky called the mother 'a reflection of her time', someone through whom he was going to attempt to trace the spiritual values of his society. He does this in the two other main sequences of which she is the protagonist: the sequence of the printing works during Stalin's Terror and that of the attempted sale of the earrings in war-time. During the Terror people were denounced and sent off to labour camps – in many cases this meant certain death. Even though the event Tarkovsky describes did not happen to his mother, stories of exile and death in labour camps abounded at that time, and everyone, Tarkovsky's mother included, lived in daily fear. In the sequence, Maria behaves with stoicism and fearlessness throughout; only when Liza verbally attacks her does she break down. The earring episode, set during the Second World War, reveals a woman who does not hesitate to humble herself in order to survive at a time of terrible deprivation; yet she also remains proud and principled, unable to ignore the display of callous affluence during such a dark time. Maria, in the end, cannot contend with the excess she is a witness to, so she flees, unable to go through with the sale. Tellingly, Tarkovsky gave his wife, Larisa, the highly unsympathetic role of the rich doctor's wife.

As noted earlier, several episodes in the script dealt with the gathering and selling of things during war-time. In these, the young boy more often than not is disapproving, ashamed and embarrassed. The person who appears to be the cause of these emotions, and the object of his hostility, is his mother. This troubled aspect of his childhood appears to have been indelibly forged in Tarkovsky's soul. And notwithstanding the words of love and praise he reserved for his mother, the director reveals a much more ambivalent relationship towards her in the film. As he explained to his comrades at the studio meetings, what was important for him was the way he *remembered* his mother, not the way she *was*. This 'remembering', however, involved a certain element of invention: Tarkovsky 're-created' his mother in the film in a way that was necessary to him. This is illustrated in the scene where, as an old woman, she knocks on the door of Alexei's flat, but fails to recognise her grandson, Ignat, who opens the door. Tarkovsky said in interview that although he did not have a logical understanding of, or explanation for, the fact that her grandson did not recognise her, he needed to see his mother's face a little frightened, a little shy, a little 'a la Dostoevsky' as he put it. 'It was very important for me to see my mother in this state. The expression of her face when she is shy, confused, disconcerted [...] It was very important for me to see this state of the soul of someone whom I feel very close to, this state of depression, of emotional awkwardness. It is like a portrait of someone in a state of humiliation.'[34] Initially, however, Tarkovsky wanted to have Ignat chase after his grandmother and have a conversation with her, which would cover the themes treated in the Pushkin letter. He explained that he later decided to drop this scene and not turn his mother into a character, in order to achieve the mood he needed for the film's final sequence.

Why would Tarkovsky want to see his actual mother – an old woman who by all accounts had a difficult time being filmed, and did it only out of love for her son – in a state of humiliation? In the same interview, Tarkovsky said he wanted to communicate a similar state when the young mother goes to sell her earrings to the rich doctor's wife. Standing in the rain, cold and wet, she attempts to take on a refined air, to justify herself. It is an absurd situation and her tone is out of place. Tarkovsky creates this same mood of bafflement and humiliation for a third time, in the scene where Liza lashes out at Maria during the printing-works sequence. Comparing her to Dostoevsky's ineffectual Maria Lebiadkina (who imagines everyone is at her beck and call but is really a victim of her husband's vicious temper), she attempts to humiliate her; she ironises Maria's 'emancipated ways', sides with her estranged husband, and predicts that she has harmed her own children. These sequences reveal a deep ambiguity in Tarkovsky over the figure of his mother. Those who knew her disagreed with his portrait of her in *Mirror*, saying she was a complex, caring and communicative woman. Yet for Tarkovsky this was perhaps a way to balance out and assuage the guilt – and resentment – he felt at the knowledge that she had sacrificed her own life and literary ambitions in order to bring up her two children, but especially Andrei, of whom she expected great things. A partial answer can perhaps be found in the disputed monologue Tarkovsky and Misharin wrote for the shooting script, which was included in the episode at the hippodrome, and was to be acted by Misharin; when that episode was cut, a small part of the monologue was given to Natalia to say in her final scene:

What relationship would you like with your mother? You cannot have the one you had in childhood, and she is right not to demand that... She's just afraid to be obtrusive [...]

You're afraid for yourself! Her intransigence, her prejudices, her stubbornness, or her belief that she knew best how to bring you up – it was because she had to exert herself, to close herself in, otherwise everything would fall apart, and she would not have coped [...]

Until you die you will not forgive her the fact that she destroyed her life for you. Yet, she is ready to forgive you everything. But you don't need her forgiveness, it's humiliating [...] She only wants one thing – for you to become a child again, so that she can hold you in her arms, cuddle you when you wake up crying, and protect you all through life.

We choose women, too, that they might love us as we were loved once, unconditionally, that they might protect us as best they can.

Despite his deep feelings of gratitude towards his mother, Tarkovsky, in growing up, also felt oppressed by her will, her nervousness, her principles and her pride. Their poverty was a source of embarrassment to him, his mother's total absence of interest in material things a source of awkward surprise. He was a witness to her struggles, aware that she, a woman by nature maladjusted to daily life, had to shoulder the weight of bringing up two young children alone. And he felt her loyalty to his father, whom she loved to the end of her days, never admitting another man into her life. She never made her children the battleground of her failed marriage, instilling in them instead a deep love and respect for their father and his art. Tarkovsky said that one of his first memories of his parents was of his father typing away, and every so often asking his mother which word to use in a particular line of poetry. He usually followed her advice. The two had met while studying together at the Literary Institute in Moscow, love of literature being their common ground. Her friends called Maria 'Tolstoy in a skirt', but she felt that she lacked the talent to be a writer. Love and motherhood put paid to her literary ambitions, but did not prevent Arseni from becoming a renowned poet. In Tarkovsky's consciousness a woman is a creator only in as far as she bears children; her inner world is connected to a man's inner world; she is called to dissolve inside him, to serve and protect him – if necessary to sacrifice herself for him. She can never, and must never attempt to, be his equal, yet she can surpass him in her ability to love. Clearly, for Tarkovsky, his mother's unquestioning and un-conditional love for his father influenced the rest of his life. His own first wife, though following his mother's fate, did not possess her mother-in-law's self-effacing, generous love, and she occasionally used their son to punish Tarkovsky for his desertion. Tarkovsky's guilt towards her would have been exacerbated by his early experience of his own mother's suffering and hardship, and he includes her in *Mirror*, which is a film not only about memory, but also about con-science and the purging of guilt. But he does not treat her with the same reverence and love reserved for his mother, albeit racked with contradictions. If the mother is immortal, because she has carried her cross with dignity and sacrificed herself, the wife is neurotic, confused and selfish; she lacks integrity. The duality of Leonardo's portrait of Ginevra de Benci (see 'Culture and History', p. 59) also symbolises the images of the mother and wife in Tarkovsky's psyche – the former enchanting, the latter repelling.

Childhood

In his last interview, when asked about the theme of childhood and its role in his work, Tarkovsky said that he never especially set out to examine it, and that we tend to give too much importance to childhood. He took issue with psychoanalysis, which sets out to explain away people's behaviour by referring to their childhood, and especially criticised the way art is oversimplified by using this approach. Yet in previous interviews Tarkovsky spoke of childhood as the most important thing for him, as the time which determined his future life, especially in connection with his art:

When I think about my childhood, I think about a time when my whole life was still ahead of me, when I felt that I was immortal and that everything was possible. Sometimes, when I ponder the fact that childhood has gone I lose myself a little. I don't know whether it has gone, or whether it's stayed with me. I fear that the *feeling*, the *sense* of childhood has gone, but not childhood itself. I think it has become the foundation, the basis of my creativity. Everything that propels me

22. Maria Tarkovskaia with Andrei and Marina, Ignatievo, 1935.
(Photograph: Lev Gornung)

to create was instilled in me in childhood. I think that if I had forgotten it, I would have been barren.[35]

Childhood in *Mirror* is mostly a place of adversity, loss and muteness. Although the narrator speaks longingly about the house of his childhood, which is a lyrical, harmonious space, the childhood dreams reveal a darker, more threatening reality. A muffled tone of fear, of imminent catastrophe, weaves a thread throughout all of Tarkovsky's films. It begins with the first frames of *Ivan's Childhood* – an earthly Garden of Eden which Ivan dwells in and which is abruptly brought to an end with a violent burst of artillery fire, killing his mother and blackening his life for ever. In his dreams, the young Alexei in *Mirror* is always on the periphery – alone, left out, searching, startled. It is only the waking memories of the dacha that offer respite. The older, war-time Alexei is a sullen, broody boy. We do not know much of what he is thinking or feeling; we catch the scolding, angry look he gives his mother when they arrive at the rich doctor's house and the confused, tormented expression on his face as he hugs his soldier father. At the shooting range, he masks his awkwardness with brashness – the military instructor is, after all, his rival in the red-head's affections. His counterpart, Ignat, is most often startled: by his father's questions, by the appearance of the mysterious women, by the sudden electric shock when he touches the spilled contents of his mother's bag. We learn that he is a mediocre student and that his father wants to send him to a military academy. Both his parents show exasperation towards him, his father for leafing through his books and starting a fire in the courtyard (accompanied by a mocking remark to the effect that he could never witness the biblical 'burning bush'), his mother for not helping her gather her things fast enough.

The most compelling child in the film is Asafiev, the young orphan at the shooting range. In some respects, he is a distillation of the countless children we have seen in the Spanish footage, children boarding the ship that will take them to the Soviet Union and away from their brutal civil war. The footage shows us endless scenes of leave-taking; parents and children kissing, crying, walking about with their belongings, looking lost and confused. The last image is of a little girl smiling, holding a doll. She turns around and suddenly notices the camera. Her smile gives way to a look of complete bewilderment and sober surprise. In those few frames, we witness the abrupt shedding of childhood. Asafiev's expression is the natural conclusion of this moment. He is caught inside a terrible vortex of loss. We learn that he is a 'Leningrader, from the blockade'. The siege of Leningrad, the longest and most vicious in the Second World War, turned people into cannibals in their attempts to survive. Corpses lay everywhere on the streets, turning the city into an open grave – scenes Asafiev would have witnessed. Asafiev does a 360-degree turn when the order 'about turn' is given. He is painfully defiant when the instructor rebukes him. When the man tells him he will send him to his parents, his dull face shows no pain. When he leaves, after the episode with the dummy grenade, tears trickle down his face, as frozen as the landscape around him. This is how this moment is described in the script: 'The difficulty of the ascent had not relieved him of his shame. The small town was multiplied and washed away by the tears that filled his eyes. Further off, beyond the river, the few reference points of the snowy Russian plains receded into indistinctness, and the whole twilight December world was, for Asafiev, a valley of cruelty, hopelessness and vengeance.'[36] Yet in the film, in an

23. The orphan Asafiev (Yuri Sventikov). (Photograph: Vladimir Murashko)

act of compassion and faith, Tarkovsky allows him a moment of respite, a small epiphany, in the image of a bird which comes and sits on his head, like a blessing.[37] When he lived in Iurievets during the war, Tarkovsky learnt to fire a rifle, though there was no shell-shocked military instructor present. One day a boatload of children from Leningrad stopped there for a few days, on their way down the Volga. It was impossible to forget their terrified, emaciated faces. Thirty years later, he created this episode, as a reminder of the terrible price war exacts on the human spirit.

Word and Image

In *Mirror*, Tarkovsky's visual poetic sensibility concurred with his father's verbal poetic sensibility, to create one of the most successful marriages of word and image in the director's work. Poetry was present in the earliest version of the script of *A White, White Day*. Its epigraph is a fragment of a Pushkin poem, written in answer to a request to inscribe his name in the album of a Polish beauty:

> What need have you of my name?
> …
> But on a day of sorrow, in the silence,
> Utter my name with melancholy.
> Say: there is a memory of me,
> In this world a heart in which I live.

The poem, like the film, speaks of the importance of memory, and of the need to be remembered. To utter someone's name is to acknowledge their existence; and if they have been long forgotten and removed from memory, it is to give them new life. It is a fitting epigraph for a film that gives new life not only to a family's past, but also to an array of historical events by connecting them to this one family's. This epigraph to the script echoes what became the film's epigraph – the healing of the stutterer. To speak is also to remember. Halting speech blocks being and therefore blocks memory; but the ability to speak 'loudly and clearly, freely and easily' as the healer requests of the boy, restores his place in the world, empowers him with the fundamental means of expression.

The script contains a fragment from another Pushkin poem, *The Prophet*.[38] Though this poem is an allusion to Isaiah, it has been interpreted as charging the poet with a mission: like the prophet, he must spread the word of God, and tell of what he knows. This interpretation supports Tarkovsky's belief that the artist *is* a prophet, a vessel carrying the will and inspiration of God, whose duty it is to give expression to the truths he is able to grasp. These poems, and the ones by Arseni Tarkovsky that follow, both in the script and in the film, map out an inner territory, deepen some of the clusters of ideas and emotions that Tarkovsky wanted to communicate. It would be spurious to draw concrete parallels between the poems, events and images that take place on screen; poetry is at once as oblique as it is precise. Tarkovsky adds poetry to the image as he might add reverberation to a sound, to deepen and multiply its effect. The poetry in *Mirror* brings a new quality into being, *transforming* rather than *explaining* the unfolding events. At the same time, it creates a parallel world of images through words. Tarkovsky uses them, as he does the music, in order to extend the life of the film outside the boundaries of the film frame.

Tarkovsky's father wrote, and reads, all four poems heard in the film. In his lectures, Tarkovsky said that the poems were not illustrative, but that they were written at the time of one or another of the episodes and are inseparable from the heroine. He gives as an example the 'poem about love' as he calls it, referring to the first poem we hear, *First Meetings* (1962), saying that the heroine remembers it at the time it was written, in 1937. In fact, the only poem written specifically at that time, in that place, and about Tarkovsky's mother, is *Ignatievo Forest* (1935). It appears in the early versions of the script, but is replaced by *First Meetings* in the published script and is not included in the film.[39] The poem talks directly about the mounting problems between Tarkovsky's parents: 'The entire forest lives in just such irritation/ as you and I have lived for this year past'. It is unclear why Tarkovsky would have given this incorrect information to his students. The poems are, indeed, more than merely illustrative; they are deeply embedded in the fabric of the film, and in the heroine's inner world (only one poem, *Life, Life* [1965] is not directly linked to her). Perhaps Tarkovsky needed to believe that they pertained to that time and that person; that, too, was part of the creative process, gathering and organising the material on a deeper, more intuitive level, making this film so rich, if not always transparent. Arseni Tarkovsky's disembodied voice has an added poignancy in a film where his absence is felt so intensely by the protagonists and by the author's consciousness. His complex artistic sensibility towers over the lives of his wife and son, revealing his elevated place in their lives.

First Meetings [Pervye svidaniia] is indeed 'a poem about love'. We hear it after the brief meeting with the doctor, having learnt from the narrator that Maria is waiting for someone else: 'If a man turned towards the house, then it was father. If he didn't, it wasn't father, and it meant that he was never coming back.' The poem maps out the blissful realm of love. The words 'epiphany', 'transfiguration', 'blessings', communicate a sense of the sacredness and profundity around this love; the woman sits on a throne holding a crystal sphere of the world in her hand, like a goddess-tsarina. Miraculous cities come into being and everything surrounding the lovers – the animate

24. Arseni and Maria Tarkovsky at the Gorchakovs' dacha in happier days, summer 1935.

and inanimate kingdoms – is alive and vibrant and responds to them. But the poem's ecstatic movement through a magical domain ends on an ominous note: 'When Fate was following in our tracks/ Like a madman with a razor in his hand'. This final image is a forewarning of love's bitter end. It echoes a line from Ignatievo Forest, 'You know how love resembles a threat', subsequently changed to 'all of our past resembles a threat'. The camera registers elements of the world found in the poem: the tsarina-mother and her realm, the lilac, the pitcher and basin, the water. Yet by the end, Maria is weeping. The poem's dark foreboding is consolidated by the next scene – the fire in the shed – witnessed dispassionately. This fire is a cipher of the poem's closing lines and we know that it returns to haunt Maria later, at another difficult moment, linking her state of mind, her loneliness and her ordeal with the sequences in the house by Ignatievo forest. Throughout the film, Tarkovsky returns to certain images, in this way creating great montage cycles of emotion, action and stillness. The three major episodes with the mother are interwoven with the father's poetry. Each poem returns us to her inner life and to her emotional and mental state in the sequence of events.

The next poem, *From morning on I waited yesterday* [S utra ia tebia dozhidalsia vchera, 1941], comes towards the end of the printing-works episode, which can be contrasted to the film's epigraph, where the boy gains the freedom to speak. Here we witness a time when people could not speak freely, when a word misplaced or mis-spelled meant possible death.[40] Everything is veiled and oblique in this sequence: the young assistant's whimpering about 'such a publication',[41] Maria's peculiar exchange with her boss: 'Do you think I'm afraid?', 'I know you're not afraid. Let others be afraid. Some will work and some will be afraid.' His reply rings like a veiled threat to anyone present who might want to interfere or even denounce the woman. Tension mounts, but inwardly, mutely, it is not externalised. We hear the poem after the worst is over. Maria is walking down a long corridor, smiling faintly, looking about. Her state of mind is indecipherable. The poem speaks of an inopportune meeting, ending with the words: 'You cannot soothe things with a word, nor wipe things away with a handkerchief.'

The corridor Maria walks down is at the Mosfilm studios and connects two of its largest buildings. Tarkovsky transforms it into a ritual passage from an outer to an inner world. The poem gives evidence of this world, and of the dissonance between its protagonists (who, for Tarkovsky, are *a priori* his mother and father). The dissonance is both emotional and temporal; the timing is wrong, the circumstances are wrong, and even the weather testifies to this. The last line fixes a deeper truth – that some things leave indelible marks. The corridor is white and bright after the artificially lit rooms filled with the black printing machines in the previous scenes. But its lightness is as deceptive as the woman's soft smile, for the poem bespeaks a grief that she will never be rid of. Just as a possible mistake in the proofs could not have been reversed, with severe consequences, so she lives inwardly with just as severe consequences from a love that was not saved, and a wound that can never heal.

The release of tension in this sequence comes through Liza's 'Dostoevskian' attack. Both women begin to cry, and Maria ends the unexpected confrontation by going to take a shower. After her attempted reconciliation, Liza skips away, ironically quoting the first line from Dante's *Purgatory*: 'Half way through my earthly life I lost my way in a gloomy forest'. In the context of this scene this line is directed at Maria; yet it is also Tarkovsky being self-referential. The two actresses later conducted a 'literary' argument through their respective memoirs. Terekhova told Tarkovsky that the episode, which originally ended with her going to take a shower after her ordeal was over, lacked something. He returned some time later with the scene of the argument. Alla Demidova (Liza),[42] who was unhappy with her performance, finding it monotonous and superficial, said that Tarkovsky just wanted the women to shed a few tears in that scene, because a close-up of a person in tears is always emotional and natural. Terekhova pointedly disputes this, suggesting that what he wanted from Demidova was to see the self-assured person she is in a state of confusion and perplexity. For Terekhova, the scene is about two cultivated, well-read women, coping with this terrible time in the only way they knew and loved – literature.

The poem *Life, Life* [Zhizn', Zhizn', 1965] is a verbal expression of the fundamental ideas in *Mirror* – immortality, roots, the cyclical and simultaneous nature of time and our duty to life. It accompanies the Sivash footage, Tarkovsky's cherished discovery, which he pronounced 'sacred' and called the heart of his film. This poem is the place where Tarkovsky father and son merge most intensely in their artistic consciousness, for it speaks of the energy and will of the creator: 'I will call up any century, go into it and build myself a house'. Alluding to the mythical Atlas, the poet props the past up on his shoulder, can measure time, and walk through it as though it was a landscape. What the poet achieves in words, his son effects through images. The poem triumphantly asserts 'on earth there is no death. All are immortal. All is immortal'. (Many years later, the hero of *The Sacrifice* will tell his young son the same thing.) These lines give context and meaning to the images of the exhausted soldiers, ennobling their struggle. As they wade through the water, carrying their rifles and pulling the heavy cannon, we hear: 'All of us are on the seashore now, and I am one of those who haul the nets when a shoal of immortality comes in'. The poem coincides with and transfigures the image at this point. It ends as we watch the tearful, but whistling Asafiev walk up the hill. The poem also unfolds across a vast landscape, and its protagonist, the artist, is like a giant striding across it – fearless, free. But in the end, despite his taming of fate and his wish for a safe, warm place, he is led – compelled – by 'life's flying needle' through the world. This paradoxical image echoes an earlier one, 'Live in the house and the house will stand', whose dissonance in respect of the Tarkovsky men's lives we have already noted. *Life, Life* is really a poem about art, because only in its realm can we perform the exalted deeds it admonishes. In this respect, it is a mirror image of *Mirror.*

We hear the last poem, *Eyrydice* [Evridika, 1961] at the end of the earring sequence. Maria and Alexei have just left the doctor's house. The poem accompanies them and continues into the last dream, where the wind escapes from the forest for the last time, and the boy Alexei runs into the room with the hanging curtains. This is by far the most hermetic poem in the film, and the most contrapuntal to the image. It tells of a dissonance between body and soul, the latter feeling captured inside the former, but unable to have purpose and direction without it. In a sense, the attempted sale of the earrings is about keeping body and soul together. Maria's hasty flight is her soul rebelling against what she has seen, momentarily unfettered from the malnourished body. The poem's last verse urges the child not to lament Eyrydice, now beyond reach, but to keep moving through the world as long as the earth responds even with the slightest sound to his every step. It returns us to the realm of childhood where everything is still in the future and there is abundant hope, resonating with the film's final sequence and the boy Alexei's buoyant cry. Like the other poems, it takes us to an associative space which lies beyond the film but which simultaneously links up with images from it: the notion of Maria as Eyrydice; a spiritous and shadowless soul – like the wind/father roaming through the film – that leaves lilac on the table to be remembered by. *Mirror* is pitched between two distinct, yet complementary, artistic sensibilities. Tarkovsky is in creative dialogue with the resonant world bequeathed to him by the absent father.

25. Maria Tarkovskaia in Zavrazhe, 1932. (Photograph: Lev Gornung)

A Profound Paradox

'Tarkovsky was unable to preserve, inviolable, the image of the paternal home as a salutary refuge,' wrote Olga Surkova, in an article exploring the autobiographical motifs in the director's work.[43] Never himself knowing a safe, stable paternal home that would counteract the threatening, unpredictable outside world – especially the one which his generation was exposed to, dominated by war and its destruction of human values – he was unable to create his own in life. In 1970 Tarkovsky attempted to create this idealised home, buying a house in the village of Miasnoe with his second wife. He set about transforming it into the lost, symbolic home of his childhood – a sanctuary where he could find peace, harmony and protection from the world. He even contemplated moving there permanently and taking up writing if directing work proved too difficult to sustain under the conditions at Mosfilm. In conversation with Guerra, Tarkovsky said: 'While the house stands, we will always live there. It is a celebration of the soul, a feast of the heart. That is what that house is. And if it is ever taken away from me then I will have nothing left on this earth.'[44] But it was Tarkovsky who 'abandoned' the house when he flew to Italy to make *Nostalgia* in 1982. He was never to return to Russia. In varying ways, his last three films chart the degrees of disenchantment at his own failure to 'live in the house'.

In *Mirror* Tarkovsky called up his century, walked into it and re-erected there the house of his childhood. In the process, he incorporated some of the important events of his country and of the times, attempting to fill in the greater picture. The house of his childhood grew in size and meaning until it incorporated his home-land, and the world. And yet when *Mirror* was completed Tarkovsky did not feel that he was free. Though the recurring dreams stopped, what came to take their place was a terrible emptiness. This emptiness was foreseen by a diary entry on 8 December 1973, after a trip to Iurievets, where he intended to film the shooting-range episode:

> I shouldn't have gone to Iurievets. It would have lived in my memory as a beautiful, happy country – the birthplace of my childhood. I was correct to write in the script of the film I am now making that we

should not return to the ruins. How empty I feel in my soul! How sad! So I have lost one more illusion, perhaps the most important one for the preservation of peace and quiet in my soul. I have buried my childhood home with my film.[45]

As Tarkovsky explained to his students, when the dreams, memories and sensations of childhood stopped visiting him, he felt as though he lost himself in a certain sense. Nothing came to take the place of those emotions, something he had foreseen in the original script where he wrote: 'The fragile joy we had felt on returning slowly ebbs from our hearts, like the blood of one mortally wounded; leaving a bitter, anguished emptiness [...] You should never return to ruins, whether it be a town, the house where you were born, or someone you have separated from.'[46] However, what had begun as a mere need to free himself of painful memories had turned into a film about something completely different. '*Mirror* was not an attempt to talk about myself, not at all. It was about my feelings towards people dear to me; about my relationship with them; my perpetual pity for them and my own inadequacy – my feeling of duty left unfulfilled.'[47]

It is a paradox that *Mirror*, a film which confirms the deep and unbreakable ties between people, between the generations, between the personal and the political, between ourselves and the world, is essentially a film about people who fail to communicate, who have failed to communicate. All the characters share that plight – they are tongue-tied, they stutter; overwhelmed by emotion they speak in quotes, obliquely; disheartened, they take flight. Yet, through sheer will, talent, faith and the miraculous transformation of art, the film achieves what Tarkovsky always strove for: 'In one form or another all my films have made the point that people are not alone and abandoned in an empty universe, but are linked by countless threads with the past and the future; that as each person lives his life he forges a bond with the whole world, indeed with the whole history of mankind.'[48] Stranded on the planet of Solaris, trying to make contact with its mysterious ocean, Snaut, one of the worn-out, tormented scientists, says: 'We don't need other worlds. We need a mirror. What man needs is man.' *Mirror* is Tarkovsky's testament to this.

Notes

1. O. Surkova, *Kniga sopostavlenii* (Moscow, 1991), p. 101.

2. A. Tarkovsky, *Sculpting in Time. Reflections on the Cinema* (London, 1986), pp. 131–2 and 136–8.

3. See also what he has to say about the Japanese concept of *saba* in connection with this, in ibid., p. 59.

4. A. Tarkovskii, 'Zapechatlennoe vremia', *Iskusstvo kino*, 4, 1967, p. 72.

5. Tarkovsky, *Sculpting in Time*, p. 21.

6. Ibid., p. 72.

7. This is a personification of an image from the poem *Song*.

8. Tarkovsky, *Sculpting in Time*, p. 78.

9. Initially, fewer poems were going to be used in the film but Feiginova had kept the recordings that had been made, not wanting to throw 'such poetry' away. Mentioned in M. Turovskaia, *7 1/2 ili fil'my Andreia Tarkovskogo* (Moscow, 1991), p. 147.

10. Tarkovsky, *Sculpting in Time*, p. 162.

11. A. Misharin, 'Na krovi, kul'ture i istorii …', in *O Tarkovskom* (Moscow, 1989), p. 64.

12. It is interesting to note here that while Western audiences see Tarkovsky as a profoundly Russian director, many Russians believe that his recognition in the West is mainly due to his European sensibility.

13. Tarkovsky, *Sculpting in Time*, p. 108.

14. Moscow was in mourning after this catastrophe and it is said that Stalin himself carried an urn with the remains of one of the ballonists.

15. Tarkovsky, *Sculpting in Time*, p. 130.

16. A. Tarkovskii, 'Ispoved' Andreia Tarkovskogo', *Kontinent*, 42, 1984, p. 387.

17. This is a personal reference, as Tarkovsky's father had wanted him to attend the academy, hoping he might be taught discipline there. In *Ivan's Childhood*, Ivan is told he is to be sent there.

18. Tarkovsky, *Sculpting in Time*, p. 212.

19. A. Tarkovskii, 'Andrei Tarkovskii o tvorchestve i o sebe', *Russkaia mysl*, 1 August 1986, pp. 12, 14.

20. Quoted in Gaston Bachelard, *Water and Dreams* (Dallas, 1983), p. 31. A most enriching way to approach Tarkovsky's use of nature is through the writings of the French philosopher Gaston Bachelard (1880–1962). His books on the four elements attempt to illuminate their deeper functions as components of the poetic imagination. They are like psychoanalytical studies, performed with amazing intuition, imagination, breadth of reference and a childlike sense of joy and wonder on the part of their author.

21. G. Ciment (ed.), *Dossier Positif. Andrei Tarkovski* (Paris, 1988), p. 92.

22. M. Bakhtin, *The Dialogic Imagination* (Austin, 1994), p. 84. Bakhtin (1895–1975), humanist philosopher and literary theorist, was a man of great erudition and maverick intelligence. Though he wrote about literature, his ideas can be applied to a broad spectrum of human endeavour, and greatly elucidate aspects of Tarkovsky's work.

23. A phrase Bakhtin used to speak of Goethe's work.

24. Bakhtin, *The Dialogic Imagination*, p. 258.

25. M. Bakhtin, *Art and Answerability. Early Philosophical Essays* (Austin, 1990), p. 193.

26. No one knows how Tarkovsky decided upon this scene; he was, however, interested in healing and had himself attended several sessions. The therapist was Margarita Merlin, a student of Kazimir Dubrovsky, a psychotherapist from Kharkov in the Ukraine, who had worked out a method of curing speech impediments.

27. Tarkovsky, *Sculpting in Time*, p. 103.

28. A. Tarkovskii, 'Edinomyshlennik prezhde vsego', in *Sovetskie khudozhniki teatra i kino* (Moscow, 1977), p. 182.

29. V. Ushitov and V. Kuchin, '"Mosfil'm" vchera, segodnia, zavtra', *Iskusstvo kino*, 2, 1974, p. 34.

30. Bakhtin, *Art and Answerability*, p. 1.

31. Quoted in A. Tarkovsky, *Time within Time. The Diaries* (Calcutta, 1989), p. 300.

32. From an unpublished interview between Tarkovsky and Guerra held at the Institut Tarkovski in Paris.

33. Both these phrases are from Arsenii Tarkovsky's poem *Life, Life* which is heard over the Sivash footage in the film.

34. Interview with A. Tarkovsky, 'Vstat' na put'', *Iskusstvo kino*, 2, 1989, p. 111.

35. A. Tarkovskii, 'Ispoved' Andreia Tarkovskogo', *Kontinent*, 42, 1984, p. 387.

36. A. Tarkovsky, *Collected Screenplays* (London, 1999), p. 298.

37. Three different sources are given for this event: Misharin one day told Tarkovsky that, when he was a child, birds used to land on his head. Tarkovsky mentioned that when his wife Larisa walked in the woods, birds came to sit on her hands. Tarkovsky's beloved film director Alexander Dovzhenko once wrote that he was becoming so good that birds came to sit on his white hair.

38. See Tarkovsky, *Collected Screenplays*, pp. 265–6.

39. For an English translation of *Ignatievo Forest*, and all the poems in *Mirror* see Tarkovsky, *Sculpting in Time*, pp. 161, 101, 123, 143, 157.

40. In the film we are never told what the imagined mistake was, but it is said to be based on a reputed incident, when Stalin's name was mis-

spelled as Sralin (from the verb 'to shit'), which some Soviet viewers would have been aware of. Tarkovsky's sister has said that their mother did once make a mistake, which was not political.

41. In the early versions of the script, the publication was referred to as 'The Collected Works', implying those of Stalin. The bureaucrats had this cut, but the political importance of the publication is implied by the young assistant's frightened reaction. Although a mistake in any official publication was considered a crime, certain publications were treated with particular attention.

42. Demidova had been rejected by Tarkovsky for the part of Hari in *Solaris* and was taken on to play Liza in *Mirror*, after Alisa Freidlikh (the wife in *Stalker*) was unavailable for the part.

43. O. Surkova, 'Avtobiograficheskie motivy v tvorchestve Andreia Tarkovskogo', *Kinovedcheskie zapiski*, 9, 1991, p. 192.

44. From the unpublished interview between Tarkovsky and Guerra.

45. From the unpublished Russian transcript of Tarkovsky's diary.

46. Tarkovsky, *Collected Screenplays*, p. 313.

47. Tarkovsky, *Sculpting in Time*, p. 134.

48. Ibid., p. 206.

4. The Reception of the Film

The earliest critical appraisal of *Mirror* took place on 13 November 1974, when members of Mosfilm were asked to comment on the film and cast their vote for first or second category. This was a standard procedure whose result would affect the film's distribution – the number of prints and cinemas it would be projected in. Sizov opened the meeting saying that the Fourth Creative Unit proposed the film be released as first category. Kremnev, as the unit's artistic director, was asked to speak first. He praised the film, and defended Tarkovsky against the accusations of elitism that had been levelled at him the previous day. He conceded that *Mirror* was complex and difficult, and that it would undoubtedly have its opponents, but concluded that it deserved the highest appraisal. Opinions varied. For some, the film was harmonious and crystal clear; others found it depressing and unfocused. Some people took issue with the quotes (the Pushkin letter and burning bush), claiming that even a cultured audience would not understand them; others were unhappy with the documentary footage and the use of the poetry. The film was pronounced Felliniesque, and anguished. One woman said the characters' uncommunicativeness and lack of understanding of each other was influenced by films from the bourgeois West. Some present hailed *Mirror* as a true work of art, whose challenging language would be understood better by future generations. Others regretted that Tarkovsky's talent did not reach out to the nation at large, but only to a select few. The major point of contention was whether the audience would understand the film and many people based their votes on that.

Sizov closed the meeting with a prolonged, disapproving speech. He disagreed with the view that this was a new step for Tarkovsky who, he was convinced, was not moving in the right direction, and pronounced the film a complete failure. He reminded people that they worked in a studio, within a collective, and for a Soviet audience. This was Mosfilm, after all, through whose productions people judged the artistic level and tendencies of Soviet cinematography and Soviet artists working in film; this was not an experimental studio where people cast about for new formal possibilities. He said films should be addressed to the nation at large, not only to cinephiles. He accused Tarkovsky of absconding from the original proposal and explained that he would vote for second category, because art, after all, should not be divorced from the requirements and objectives of the times. There were eleven votes for first category, twelve votes for second. *Mirror* was to be, as the critic Valeri Fomin called it in his article on its fraught history, 'a masterpiece of the second category'.[1]

As if this was not enough, *Mirror* was one of four films discussed in a 'friendly', open session between the leadership of the Union of Cinematographers and the board of Goskino. The other three films were Andrei Konchalovsky's *Romance for Lovers* [Romans o vliublennykh, 1974], Iuli Karasik's *The Hottest Month* [Samyi zharkii mesiats, 1974] and Andrei Smirnov's *Autumn*. As these were films on so-called 'contemporary themes', the bureaucrats, aided by scriptwriters, critics and directors (Konchalovsky, notably, among them) thought it topical to 'discuss' them in conjunction with the latest directive on cinema from the Central Committee of the Communist Party, titled 'On the measures for the future development of Soviet cinema'. *Autumn* and *Mirror* became the sacrificial lambs of this show trial, designed to appease the higher echelons of the Party. *Mirror* was again criticised for its inaccessibility, for being a monologue rather than a dialogue, and for failing to draw conclusions or present a clearly outlined idea. A few dissenting voices spoke of Tarkovsky's unique talent, of his courage in taking a confessional tone and of pushing the boundaries of form. One even conceded that this was a film about his own thoughts and memories. Yet all, in the end, pronounced the film a failure. A letter sent to the Central Committee of the Communist Party, written by Boris Pavlenok, reads in part:

> All the speakers noted the creative failure Andrei Tarkovsky had in *Mirror*. The original script had led us to expect a poetic and patriotic film about the hero's childhood and boyhood, which coincided with the years of the Great Patriotic War, and about the formation of the artist. This original intention, however, was only partly realised. Overall, the director created an utterly subjective work in conception and mood, mannered and artificial in its cinematic language, and highly incomprehensible. His disregard of his audience, expressed through complicated symbolism and a vagueness of ideas, totally breaking with the best realist trends of Soviet cinema, was especially criticised [...] Taking into account that *Mirror* and *Autumn* constitute examples of obvious artistic failure, Goskino has decided to release these films in limited copies.[2]

Mirror was not given an official première, nor did Ermash allow it to go to the Cannes film festival, ostensibly because he feared it might win a prize. It was released on 7 March 1975, without publicity or posters, and shown in two cinemas on the outskirts of Moscow. People queued for hours to get in, but there were many who walked out of the screening. Tarkovsky received an unprecedented number of letters from viewers, some insulting, baffled or dismissive. Those that were complementary took the form of ecstatic confessions. He later said it was these letters that supported his decision to continue making films. After the publication of the 'show trial' in *Iskusstvo kino*,[3] the leading film magazine, the press was silent. Two sympathetic articles by film critics Victor Demin and Maia Turovskaia were withdrawn on the eve of their publication and there was an official ban on reviews. The authorities tried to bury the film, taking it out of the cinemas quickly, refusing to distribute it within the Soviet Union and to sell it abroad, despite frequent requests. Articles began to appear in the Soviet press several years after the film's release. Some found *Mirror* deliberately complicated and mannered, others were admiring of its unusual and individual language, attempting to unravel its fragmentary nature, its merging of different realities and the significance of the title. Many gave special attention to Arseni Tarkovsky's poetry, not only within the context of *Mirror*, but in respect of Tarkovsky's entire cinematic output. Those who belonged to Tarkovsky's generation identified with his depiction of the childhood world and its familiar objects, even the mother's dress, a common design obtained with coupons in the pre-war years. And though Soviet critics had no problems recognising the subtext of many episodes – the 'Terror', the resonances of war, the Spaniards' presence in the film, and the familiar documentary footage – they were surprised with Tarkovsky's boldness at using the first person singular as the foundation of the film. His approach evoked rapture or outrage; it was the first time a Soviet film was so overtly personal, both in word and image.

Mirror was screened in Paris in 1978 and in London in 1980. Its first English-language review was by Herbert Marshall in *Sight and Sound* (Spring 1976). As it was based on a single viewing, in an uncomfortable Leningrad cinema, it contains several errors about the characters and confuses some of the time frames. This is a common problem, also experienced by some Soviet critics, which occurs in several of the English-language interpretations of the film. Although Western critics would have been more exposed to experimental and auteur cinema, with its particular 'stamp', and therefore more seasoned in non-linear narrative, they found it difficult to contend with Tarkovsky's polyphonic canvas. Often, they did not grasp the deeper significance of the episodes, because they were unaware of their historical and cultural context. Inadequate translations also hindered understanding, as did having to take in the image while reading often inaccurate renditions of the highly complex poetry. Of the English-language books, the most elaborate and precise on *Mirror* is Johnson and Petrie's, which also provides an overview of the main critical responses to the film, in Russia and abroad. Peter Green's book has an interesting chapter on the film, while Kovács and Szilágyi's is the most culturally resonant. Turovskaia's analysis of *Mirror* is the only one by a Russian critic available in English, but her book has been heavily edited, leaving out many nuances and extensive interviews with some of Tarkovsky's closest collaborators, which provide fascinating details on his working methods. Vlada Petrić has written an excellent article on Tarkovsky's dream imagery, focusing on *Mirror* and *Stalker*. Director Olivier Assayas makes some fascinating observations on the film, in conversation with Bérénice Reynaud.

In *Sculpting in Time* Tarkovsky writes: 'Anyone who wants can look at my films as into a mirror, in which he will see himself.' For many people *Mirror* has proven the most intimate and complex of Tarkovsky's seven 'mirrors'. In the end, the film's very structure and timeless quality will always resist analysis and explanation. And there is a sense in which it does not really matter whether we have a full understanding of all the levels, subtexts and characters included in it. Those who can merge with *Mirror*'s sensibility and rhythm will reap the rewards, regardless of how much they know. Every time they return to it, as to a favourite book or piece of music, they will divine yet another piece of the inexhaustible puzzle. Today, a quarter of a century after the making of *Mirror*, and with the cumulative effect of exposure to experimental films, audiences are less likely to be baffled by its structure. Yet, when all is said and done, this film works on the heart and soul, not the mind; it is with them, first and foremost, that we must approach it.

Notes

1. Quoted in the article of the same name by V. Fomin, 'Shedevr vtoroi kategorii', *Literaturnaia gazeta,* 13, 25 March 1992, p. 8.
2. Quoted in ibid.
3. 'Glavnaia tema – sovremennost'', *Iskusstvo kino*, 3, 1975, pp. 1–18.

Further Reading

Writings by Tarkovsky

Collected Screenplays (London, 1999)
Sculpting in Time. Reflections on the Cinema (London, 1986)
Time within Time. The Diaries (Calcutta, 1991)
Journal 1970–1986 (Paris, 1993)
Uroki rezhissury [Lessons in Directing] (Moscow, 1993)
'Vstat' na put'' [Follow the Road], *Iskusstvo kino*, 2, 1989, pp. 109–29

Studies on Tarkovsky

Assayas, O., 'Tarkovsky. Seeing is Believing', *Sight and Sound*, January 1997, pp. 24–5.
Ciment, G. (ed.), *Dossier Positif. Andrei Tarkovski* (Paris, 1988)
de Baecque, A., *Andrei Tarkovski* (Paris, 1989)
Dempsey, M., 'Lost Harmony. Tarkovsky's *The Mirror* and *Stalker*', *Film Quarterly*, 35, Fall 1981, pp. 12–17
Estève, M. (ed.), *Andrei Tarkovski* (Paris, 1986)
Gauthier, G., *Andrei Tarkovski* (Paris, 1988)
Graffy, J., 'Tarkovsky. The Weight of the World', *Sight and Sound*, January 1997, pp. 18–22
Green, P., *Andrei Tarkovsky. The Winding Quest* (London, 1993)
Johnson, V. and G. Petrie, 'Tarkovsky', in D. J. Goulding (ed.), *Five Film-makers* (Bloomington and Indianapolis, 1994), pp. 1–49
— *The Films of Andrei Tarkovsky. A Visual Fugue* (Bloomington and Indianapolis, 1994)

Kovács, B. A. and A. Szilágyi *Les mondes d'Andrei Tarkovski* [The Worlds of Andrei Tarkovsky] (Lausanne, 1987)

Le Fanu, M., *The Cinema of Andrei Tarkovsky* (London, 1987)

Marshall, H., 'Andrei Tarkovsky's *The Mirror*', *Sight and Sound*, Spring 1976, pp. 92–5

Petric, V., 'Tarkovsky's Dream Imagery', *Film Quarterly*, 43, 2, Winter 1989–90, pp. 28–34

Sandler, A. M. (ed.), *Mir i fil'my Andreia Tarkovskogo* [The World and Films of Andrei Tarkovsky] (Moscow, 1991)

Surkova, O., *Kniga sopostavlenii* [A Book of Juxtapositions] (Moscow, 1991)

Tarkovskaia, M. (ed.), *About Andrei Tarkovsky* (Moscow, 1990)

Turovskaya, M., *Tarkovsky. Cinema as Poetry* (London, 1989)

— *7 1/2, ili fil'my Andreia Tarkovskogo* [7 1/2, or The Films of Andrei Tarkovsky] (Moscow, 1991)